AMERICAN MARTYRS

★★★★★★ **FROM 1542** ★★★★★★

Albert J. Nevins, M.M.

D0931709

Our Sunday Visitor Publishing Division
Our Sunday Visitor, Inc.
Huntington, Indiana 46750

Write: Our Sunday Visitor Publishing Division
Our Sunday Visitor, Inc.
200 Noll Plaza
Huntington, Indiana 46750

International Standard Book Number: 0-87973-488-4
Library of Congress Catalog Card Number: 86-84002

Cover Design by James E. McIlrath

PRINTED IN THE UNITED STATES OF AMERICA

488

CONTENTS

ILLUSTRATIONS

Page 22, Father Luís Cancer de Barbastro, O.P.
Florida, 1549 (NC sketch by Maggie Bunson)

Page 46, St. Isaac Jogues, S.J.
New York, 1646 (NC sketch by Maggie Bunson)

Page 97, Father Luís Jayme, O.F.M.
California, 1775 (NC sketch by Maggie Bunson)

Page 107, Archbishop Charles J. Seghers
Alaska, 1886

Page 140, Bishop Francis Xavier Ford, M.M.
China, 1947 (NC News)

Page 149, Father Casimir (Michael) Cypher, O.F.M. Conv.
Honduras, 1975 (NC News)

Page 152, Sister Maura Clarke, M.M., Sister Ita Ford, M.M.,
Sister Dorothy Kazel, O.S.U. (*NC News*), Jean Donovan
El Salvador, 1980 (Donovan photo courtesy of the
Catholic Universe Bulletin, Cleveland, Ohio)

Page 160, Father Stanley Rother, Secular
Guatemala, 1981 (NC News)

Page 165, Brother James Miller, F.S.C.
Guatemala, 1982 (NC News)

Page 168, Father John Rossiter, Secular
Wisconsin, 1985 (NC News)

Introduction:
An American Martyrology

A word at the start about the boundaries of this book. In a strict sense, according to makers of dictionaries, a martyrology is "a catalog of Roman Catholic martyrs and saints arranged by the dates of their feasts." In a broader approach, a martyrology is an ecclesiastical history treating the lives and sufferings of martyrs. It is in this latter connotation that the term is understood in this work.

When Martin Waldseemuller in 1507 first used the term "America," he was referring to the entire New World — North, Central, and South America. An American properly is any inhabitant of those three regions, despite the fact that the citizens of the United States arrogate the word for their own use. Nevertheless, here the word is being taken in its appropriated sense and applies only to the United States. The people portrayed in this book are either those who died within the borders of the United States or United States citizens who gave their lives elsewhere.

The word "martyr" should itself be explained. The Church's theology of martyrdom is rooted in Christ's observation that ". . . whoever loses his life for my sake will save it" (Lk 9:24). Martyrdom, then, implies death and not merely suffering. Some restrict the term to those who were given a choice of life or death. In this use, the martyr is presented with an alternative: giving up the Faith or giving up his head. The martyr chooses the latter. This is immediate or proximate martyrdom. There is also a mediate martyrdom, when a person stays at his or her religious task despite the threat of anti-Catholic violence and dies as the result of that choice. It is in this mediate sense that the word is used here. In this book are included those who have suffered violent death while engaged in preaching and propagating the Catholic Faith, such death being caused by *odium fidei* (hatred of the Faith).

This book has a threefold purpose: 1) to give as comprehensive list of Catholic American martyrs as can be gathered, and in doing so to present pertinent information on their lives, works, and manner of death; 2) to show that the Catholic Faith was planted in the United States at the cost of many lives; and, 3) to reveal that Americans themselves were willing to give their own lives to plant that same Faith beyond their own borders. It is true that many of our Protestant brothers and sisters died in the cause of religion, and perhaps one day someone will prepare a martyrology for them. This book, however, is concerned solely with Catholics.

Interest in our Catholic American martyrs became systematized at the annual meeting of the American bishops held in Washington, D.C., in November of 1939. Bishop John Mark Gannon, who had long been concerned with the subject, offered a motion to the bishops that a petition be presented to the Holy See introducing "one Cause for the beatification and canonization of the early missionaries who were put to death for the Faith in what is now United States territory." The motion was passed, and to prepare such a list of martyrs the Commission for the Cause of Canonization of the Martyrs of the United States (hereafter referred to in the text as CCCMUS) was formed.

Bishop Gannon was named chairman of the commission, and the other members were selected on the basis of historical competence: Father John Wynne, S.J., a historian and vice-postulator of the successful Cause of the North American Jesuit martyrs; Father Michael Kenny, S.J., whose *Romance of the Floridas* is a basic historical document; Father Marion A. Habig, O.F.M., researcher and historian of Franciscana; and later, Monsignor Peter Guilday, the recognized dean of American Catholic history. Father

6

John Powers, an aide of the bishop, was named secretary and editor.

The first task of the commission was to seek out the martyrs of the United States. Eventually a list of 116 names was adopted and a report prepared for Rome. On September 23, 1941, Cardinal Denis Dougherty of Philadelphia forwarded this list to the Sacred Congregation of Rites. Unfortunately, within a few months the United States was at war and more pressing matters took precedence. In 1948, the then Archbishop Gannon was in Europe in connection with relief work and had the opportunity of an audience with Pope Pius XII. He mentioned the martyrdom document, and the Pope told him, "The Cause is beautiful." It may be that the study by the Congregation goes on. In any event, the bishops as a body have taken no further action, and there are some modern martyrs who certainly should be added to any Roman study. This manuscript of preliminary studies by the bishops' commission is the basic source for the early sketches in this book. However, in researching these studies further, some corrections have been made in the commission's findings and new information developed. There have also been deletions. For example, entry number 38 on the bishops' list is Father René Ménard, S.J., who has been dropped in the present work. Father Ménard disappeared on a journey in Wisconsin in 1661, but there is no evidence that he met foul play or is a martyr. The *Jesuit Relations* (vol. 71, p. 144) simply states he "perished in the primitive wilderness in northeastern Wisconsin," and the bishops' text opines that perhaps he was murdered by Indians. Perhaps so, perhaps not. Without positive evidence it is better to omit him.

In drawing up a roster to be added to the original chronological list, the decision was made not to include any military chaplains, even though some of these men died in a heroic manner while attending to religious duties. The reason is that while in some cases the enemy may have been op-

7

posed to religion, in the particular cases the killing was indiscriminate, without *odium fidei* present. This same reasoning was applied to other violent deaths, such as that of Father Raymond Herman, a missionary from the Dubuque, Iowa, Archdiocese, who was murdered in his Bolivian rectory during the course of a robbery.

Finally, the author wishes to dedicate this book to the late Father Marion A. Habig, O.F.M., who became the foremost authority on Franciscan history in the United States and was a member of the original commission that prepared the initial listings. When this book was in its planning stages, the author wrote Father Marion, seeking his advice in defining martyrdom. Father Marion not only replied and gave encouragement but confessed that he had hoped someday to update the original findings. To this end, he had made some notes and references, which he graciously sent along. Many of these notes have been incorporated in this book. The author regrets that Father Marion died before the work was finished and that he was not made aware how gratefully his help was appreciated. The author also wishes to thank the many archivists, family members, and religious superiors who were so generous in answering requests for information. The author, however, assumes responsibility for all conclusions and whatever errors may have inadvertently been allowed to slip into this work.

It is to be hoped that the American bishops, who are part of a great American religious heritage, will soon again take up the furtherance of the Cause of the American martyrs. If the present work can help in any way, the effort will be more than amply repaid.

Chronological List of Martyrs of the United States

(Number refers both to order and biographical sketch. For abbreviations, see page 14.)

1.	Juan de Padilla OFM	Kansas	1542
2.	Juan de la Cruz OFM	New Mexico	1542
3.	Luís Descalona de Ubeda OFM	New Mexico	1542
4.	Diego de Peñalosa OP	Florida	1549
5.	Brother Fuentes OP	Florida	1549
6.	Luís Cancer de Barbastro OP	Florida	1549
7.	Diego de la Cruz OP	Texas	1553
8.	Hernando Méndez OP	Texas	1553
9.	Juan Ferrer OP	Texas	1553
10.	Juan de Mena OP	Texas	1553
11.	Pedro Martínez SJ	Florida	1566
12.	Luís de Quirós SJ	Virginia	1571
13.	Gabriel de Solís SJ	Virginia	1571
14.	Juan Bautista Méndez SJ	Virginia	1571
15.	Juan Bautista de Segura SJ	Virginia	1571
16.	Cristóbal Redondo SJ	Virginia	1571
17.	Gabriel Gómez SJ	Virginia	1571
18.	Pedro Linares SJ	Virginia	1571
19.	Sancho Zeballos SJ	Virginia	1571
20.	Juan de Santa María OFM	New Mexico	1581
21.	Francisco López OFM	New Mexico	1582
22.	Augustín Rodríguez OFM	New Mexico	1582
23.	Pedro de Corpa OFM	Georgia	1597
24.	Blas de Rodríguez OFM	Georgia	1597
25.	Miguel de Auñón OFM	Georgia	1597

9

26.	Antonio de Badajoz OFM	Georgia	1597
27.	Francisco Verascola OFM	Georgia	1597
28.	Pedro de Ortega OFM	New Mexico	1631
29.	Pedro Miranda OFM	New Mexico	1631
30.	Francisco Letrado OFM	New Mexico	1632
31.	Martín de Arvide OFM	Arizona	1632
32.	Francisco Porras OFM	Arizona	1633
33.	Diego de San Lucas OFM	New Mexico	1639
34.	St. René Goupil SJ	New York	1642
35.	St. Isaac Jogues SJ	New York	1646
36.	St. John Lalande SJ	New York	1646
37.	Unnamed Franciscan	Florida	1647
38.	Unnamed Franciscan	Florida	1647
39.	Unnamed Franciscan	Florida	1647
40.	Pedro Avila y Ayala OFM	New Mexico	1672
41.	Alonso Gil de Avila OFM	New Mexico	1675
42.	Bartolomé Naranjo, Indian Layman	New Mexico	1680
43.	Juan Bernal OFM	New Mexico	1680
44.	Domingo de Vera OFM	New Mexico	1680
45.	Fernando de Velasco OFM	New Mexico	1680
46.	Manuel Tinoco, OFM	New Mexico	1680
47.	Juan Bautista Pío OFM	New Mexico	1680
48.	Tomás de Torres OFM	New Mexico	1680
49.	Antonio de Mora OFM	New Mexico	1680
50.	Juan de la Pedroso OFM	New Mexico	1680
51.	Matías Rendón OFM	New Mexico	1680
52.	Luís de Morales OFM	New Mexico	1680
53.	Antonio Sánchez de Pro OFM	New Mexico	1680
54.	Francisco de Lorenzana OFM	New Mexico	1680
55.	Juan de Talbán OFM	New Mexico	1680
56.	José de Montesdoca OFM	New Mexico	1680
57.	Juan de Jesús OFM	New Mexico	1680
58.	Lucas Maldonado OFM	New Mexico	1680
59.	Juan del Val OFM	New Mexico	1680
60.	José de Espeleta OFM	Arizona	1680
61.	Augustín de Santa María OFM	Arizona	1680

62. José de Figueroa OFM	Arizona	1680
63. José de Trujillo OFM	Arizona	1680
64. Gabriel de la Ribourde OFM	Illinois	1680
65. Zenobe Membré OFM	Texas	1689
66. Maxim Le Clercq OFM	Texas	1689
67. Abbé Chefdeville SS	Texas	1689
68. Stephen Tegananokoa, Indian Layman	New York	1690
69. Frances Gonannhatenha, Indian Laywoman	New York	1692
70. Margaret Garangouas, Indian Laywoman	New York	1692
71. Francisco de Jesús María Casañas OFM	New Mexico	1696
72. José de Arbizu OFM	New Mexico	1696
73. Antonio de Carbonel OFM	New Mexico	1696
74. Francisco Corvera OFM	New Mexico	1696
75. Antonio Moreno OFM	New Mexico	1696
76. Luís Sánchez OFM	Florida	1696
77. Christopher Plunkett OFMCap	Virginia	1697
78. Nicholas Foucault MEP	Mississippi	1702
79. Juan Parga Arraiyo OFM	Florida	1704
80. Antonio Enixa, Indian Layman	Florida	1704
81. Amador Cuipa Feliciano, Indian Layman	Florida	1704
82. Domingo Criado OFM	Florida	1704
83. Tiburcio de Osorio OFM	Florida	1704
84. Augustín Ponce de León OFM	Florida	1704
85. Jean François Buisson de St. Cosmé MEP	Louisiana	1706
86. Constantine Delhalle OFM	Michigan	1706
87. Jacques Gravier SJ	Alabama	1708
88. Léonard Vatier OFM	Wisconsin	1715
89. Juan Mínguez OFM	Nebraska	1720
90. José Pita OFM	Texas	1721
91. Sebastien Rale SJ	Maine	1724

92. Luís Montés de Oca OFM	Texas	1726
93. Paul du Poisson SJ	Mississippi	1729
94. Jean Souel SJ	Mississippi	1729
95. Father Gaston MEP	Illinois	1730
96. Domingo de Saraoz OFM	New Mexico	1731
97. Antoine Senat SJ	Mississippi	1736
98. Pierre d'Artiquette, Layman	Mississippi	1736
99. François Marie Bissot de Vincennes, Layman	Mississippi	1736
100. Louis d'Ailebout de Coulonge, Layman	Mississippi	1736
101. Louis Charles du Tisne, Layman	Mississippi	1736
102. François Mariauchau d'Esgly, Layman	Mississippi	1736
103. Pierre Antoine de Tonty, Layman	Mississippi	1736
104. Louis Groston de St. Agne, Layman	Mississippi	1736
105. Jean Pierre Aulneau SJ	Minnesota	1736
106. Francisco Xavier Silva OFM	Texas	1749
107. José Francisco Ganzabal OFM	Texas	1752
108. Alonso Giraldo de Terreros OFM	Texas	1758
109. José Santiesteban Aberin OFM	Texas	1758
110. Luís Jayme OFM	California	1775
111. Juan Marcello Díaz OFM	California	1781
112. José Matías Moreno OFM	California	1781
113. Francisco Hermenegildo Garcés OFM	California	1781
114. Juan Antonio Barreneche OFM	California	1781
115. Andrés Quintana OFM	California	1812
116. Antonio Díaz de León OFM	Texas	1834
117. Francis Bassost OFMCap	California	1872
118. Charles J. Seghers, Archbishop	Alaska	1886
119. Leo Heinrich OFM	Colorado	1908
120. James Edwin Coyle, Secular	Alabama	1921
121. Patrick E. Heslin, Secular	California	1921
122. Walter Coveyou CP	China	1929
123. Clement Seybold CP	China	1929

124. Godfrey Holbein CP	China	1929
125. Gerard A. Donovan MM	China	1938
126. Robert J. Cairns MM	China	1941
127. Arthur C. Duhamel SM	Solomon Islands	1942
128. James Gerard Hennessey, Secular	Solomon Islands	1942
129. Otto A. Rauschenbach MM	China	1945
130. Benedict Jensen OFM	China	1947
131. James Maginn SSC	Korea	1950
132. Patrick T. Brennan SSC	Korea	1950
133. Patrick J. Byrne MM	Korea	1950
134. Francis Xavier Ford MM	China	1952
135. William Carl Kruegler MM	Bolivia	1962
136. Marcellus Cabo OFM	Wisconsin	1974
137. Casmir Cypher OFMConv	Honduras	1975
138. Maura Clarke MM	El Salvador	1980
139. Ita Ford MM	El Salvador	1980
140. Dorothy Kazel OSU	El Salvador	1980
141. Jean Donovan, Lay Missioner	El Salvador	1980
142. Stanley Rother, Secular	Guatemala	1981
143. James Miller FSC	Guatemala	1982
144. John Rossiter, Secular	Wisconsin	1985
145. Ferdinand Roth, Lay Minister	Wisconsin	1985
146. William Hammes, Layman	Wisconsin	1985

Abbreviations Used

OFM	Order of Friars Minor (Franciscan)
OFMCap	Order of Friars Minor Capuchin (Franciscan Capuchin)
OFMConv	Order of Friars Minor Conventual (Conventual Franciscan)
OP	Order of Preachers (Dominican)
SJ	Society of Jesus (Jesuit)
SS	Society of St. Sulpice (Sulpician)
MEP	Paris Foreign Mission Society
CP	Congregation of the Passion (Passionist)
MM	Maryknoll Missioner (Maryknoller)
SM	Society of Mary (Marist)
SSC	Society of St. Columban (Columban)
OSU	Order of St. Ursula (Ursuline)

Biographies of Martyrs
and Accounts
of Their Martyrdoms

1. Father Juan de Padilla, Franciscan (1542)
Protomartyr of the United States

When Father Marcos de Niza returned from his exploratory journey into what is now the southwestern United States, he brought back with him to Mexico a tale of seven golden cities of Cibola that he himself had seen from a distance and about which he had been told fabulous stories. The viceroy of Mexico, Antonio de Mendoza, immediately set about organizing an expedition to seek out these treasures, placing Francisco Vasquez de Coronado in charge.

In February 1540, Coronado and his troops began the march north from Compostela. Walking along with the foot soldiers was Father Juan de Padilla, a Franciscan friar, to whom expeditions were routine, since he was one of the pioneer missioners in Mexico.

Father Padilla was born in Andalusia, southern Spain, c. 1492. He joined the Franciscans and after ordination was posted to Mexico, arriving there c. 1526, only five years after the conquest by Cortez. In 1527 he is recorded as accompanying Cortez on a 300-mile expedition to Colima. Shortly after this journey he was appointed superior of a new monastery at Tulancingo, Hidalgo. In 1529 he was on the march again, this time with Nuño de Guzman. He did not go as far as Culiacan, the expedition's goal, but remained behind in

Jalisco to preach the Gospel, working in the area with great success for the next decade. He made many converts, notably a number of chiefs, and founded new Franciscan friaries. It was while engaged in this work that he was selected as one of the seven Franciscans to march north with Coronado, on what the historian Herbert Bolton has called "one of the epochal explorations of all history."

The party made its way northward along the western slope of the Sierra Madre Mountains, through the Sonora River Gorge, across the Gila River, turning east at the Indian village of Hawikuh, a Zuni pueblo. The only gold found in Cibola was the afternoon sunlight reflecting from adobe huts. Coronado dispatched some men northwest, where they discovered the Grand Canyon. Coronado pushed east into the upper Rio Grande valley to winter at Tiguex (now Bernalillo, New Mexico). The Indians, perhaps wishing to get rid of this invasion of their pueblos, told Coronado of Gran Quivira, where there was fabulous wealth. Thus, in the spring of 1541, Coronado again marched east, through the panhandles of Texas and Oklahoma, turning north into Kansas, crossing the Arkansas River, which Coronado named the River of St. Peter and Paul because it was reached on June 29, the feast day of those apostles. Coronado found no wealth in Quivira, only miserable buffalo-hide lodges of the Indians. After twenty-five days of exploration, he called a halt to the journey and decided to return to Tiguex for another winter before making the journey back to Mexico.

After planting a large wooden cross in the main village of the Quiviras, Coronado led the expedition back to Tiguex. When the spring of 1542 arrived, Coronado decided to give up his search and return to Mexico. Father de Padilla announced that he was returning to the Quiviras, since he had made them a promise that he would be back. Coronado assigned him a Portuguese soldier, Andrès Docampo, and Father Padilla chose two *donados*, or unordained missioners, Brothers Lucas and Sebastian, and several Mexican Indian boys to go with him. All in the party traveled on foot except for the mounted Docampo.

After another incredible journey through an uncharted land, Father de Padilla and his companions reached the Quivira village and found their cross still standing. They were warmly received, and all went well until autumn, when Father de Padilla announced that he was also taking his message to the neighboring Kaw tribe, enemies of the Quiviras, some of whom had no wish to share with their foes what the priest had brought them.

Nevertheless, Father de Padilla decided that the Gospel must be given to all. With his little group he set out across the prairie for the Kaws. The next day Docampo, from his perch on horseback, saw Quiviras coming in pursuit, their whoops indicating their warlike intentions. The historian Mota Padilla gives this account:

"[The friar] requested the Portuguese to flee, since the latter was on horseback, and to take with him the oblates and the boys, who, being young, were able to run and save themselves. Being defenseless, they all fled as he desired; and the blessed Father, kneeling down, offered up his life, which he sacrificed for the good of the souls of others. He thus realized his most ardent desire — the felicity of martyrdom by the arrows of these barbarians, who afterwards threw his body into a pit and covered it with innumerable rocks."

Docampo and the two Brothers were captured and held prisoner for almost a year before they could escape. It took them nearly nine years to reach the Spaniards at Tampico, Mexico, where they made known the martyrdom of Father de Padilla. Brother Lucas was later to die beneath a hail of arrows in Durango, Mexico, in 1565.

There is some dispute where the martyrdom took place, several places in Kansas, Nebraska, and the Texas Panhandle claiming the honor. The difficulty arises from determining the whereabouts of Coronado's Rio de San Pedro y San Pablo. Several have proposed the river to be the Canadian, which would bolster Texan claims. However, the best opinion makes it the Arkansas, which site is supported by the number of days various stages of the march took and Coronado's "forty degrees of latitude." This would place the main village of Quivira around Great Bend, Kansas, and the place of martyrdom near Lyons, Kansas. In 1941, the Diocese of Wichita held a pontifical celebration at Lyons to commemorate the four hundredth anniversary of the martyrdom. However, monuments to Father de Padilla have been erected in Logan Grove, Herington, Manhattan, Alma, and Council Grove. The Kansas Historical Society placed a roadside marker in Herington which says, "The exact place of his death is unknown."

(There is an old tradition that the remains of Father de Padilla were recovered and reinterred under the main altar of the mission church at Isleta, N.M., but historians believe this to be a case of mistaken identity and that the Isleta relics are those of Father Juan José Padilla, who worked in the region at the end of the seventeenth century.)

Sources:
Habig, Marion A., *The Franciscan Book of Saints*
     Heroes of the Cross
     Unpublished notes
CCCMUS,* *The Martyrs of the United States*
Northwestern Kansas Register, "Here a Padilla — There a Padilla"
  (August 16, 1974)
Bolton, Herbert E., *Coronado, Knight of Pueblo and Plains*

---

*(CCCMUS — Commission for the Cause of Canonization of the Martyrs of the United States. This Commission, composed of Church historians, prepared a report for submission to Rome by the American bishops, entitled *The Martyrs of the United States of America*. It is a basic source document, and hereinafter this report will be referred to only by the letters.)

Mota Padilla, *Historia de la Conquista de la Provincia de la Nueva Galicia*

2. Father Juan de la Cruz, Franciscan (1542)
3. Brother Luís Descalona de Ubeda, Franciscan (1542)
Protomartyrs of New Mexico

These two Franciscan missioners were among those who accompanied Coronado from Mexico. It is not clear whether or not they went with Coronado into Kansas. They may have remained behind to do missionary work in Tiguex, the expedition base in New Mexico, where a chapel had been built and Father Juan de la Cruz served as pastor.

Father Juan de la Cruz was known for his holiness. Gerónimo de Mendieta, in his *Historia Eclesiastica*, written at the end of the sixteenth century, tells his readers that Coronado held the priest "in such high esteem that he commanded his soldiers to touch their helmets whenever they heard the name of this Father mentioned."

Brother Luís was also highly regarded. Sotomayor, who was with Coronado, declared that Brother Luís seemed to be one of the most perfect Religious in the world since his life was one of perpetual prayer. Whenever the army encamped anywhere, he says, the good Brother would look for a quiet spot where he could kneel and pray without being disturbed.

When Coronado came to New Mexico from Kansas to winter at Tiguex for the second time, he planned to return to Kansas. However, in the spring of 1542 he was thrown from his horse and badly injured. As a result, he decided to go back to Mexico with his soldiers, concluding that the Seven

Cities of Gold and Gran Quivira were but figments of imagination.

Father Juan de Padilla, the superior, said that he and his four Franciscan companions would remain behind to do missionary work. Coronado tried in vain to persuade them to return with him but they were adamant. Finally, Coronado allowed the Portuguese soldier Andrés Docampo to remain with them. After Coronado left, Father de Padilla placed Father Juan de la Cruz in the church at Tiguex and sent Brother Luís to begin a parish at Pecos, thus establishing the first two missions in the present United States. Then he, Docampo, and the two Mexican lay brothers left for Quivira.

Details of what happened to the two missioners who remained behind in New Mexico are scarce. The Tiguas Indians had not been treated too well by Coronado's men, and there was resentment toward them which may have included the Franciscans. Bandelier simply tells us that Father Juan de la Cruz "disappeared." Mota Padillo is more concrete, writing in his *Historia* (p. 168): "Regarding Father Friar Juan de la Cruz we have the following notice: after he had worked for the instruction of the Indians of Tiguas and Coquite, he died pierced by Indian arrows, because all did not accept his doctrines and counsels." Vetancurt says he was killed on November 30, 1542, but this date is suspect.

Brother Luís had gone to his mission even before Coronado departed. He had built himself a small hut outside Pecos, an Indian pueblo about thirty miles southeast of today's Santa Fe. It was a pueblo of about twenty-five hundred Indians, consisting of two terraced apartment houses of four stories. Before Coronado left, he sent a party of soldiers with sheep for the Brother, who told his visitors that he was having some success but that he was getting opposition from the medicine men. He was never seen again. He was killed by Indians at the instigation of medicine men toward the end of 1542, according to best sources.

Sources:

Habig, Marion A., *Franciscan Herald* (January 1965), and unpublished notes
CCCMUS
Mendieta, Geronimo de, *Historia Ecclesiastica*
Moto Padilla, op.cit.
American Catholic Quarterly Review, Vol. XV (1890), pp. 551-565

Florida

4. Father Diego de Peñolosa, Dominican (1549)
5. Brother Fuentes, Dominican (1549)
6. Father Luís Cancer de Barbastro, Dominican (1549)
Protomartyrs of Florida

The Spanish crown was concerned with the conversion of the Indians of Florida, and the viceroy of Mexico was instructed to prepare an expedition for evangelization there. He entrusted the task to the Dominicans in Mexico, and Father Luís Cancer was assigned to head the mission. Father Cancer, from the region of Aragon in Spain, was a veteran missioner, having evangelized in the area of Guatemala. He had recently arrived back from Spain, where he had gone to raise recruits for the New World mission. His efforts were unsuccessful, as Spanish Dominican provincials had put an embargo on recruitment because the Spanish *conventos* were being decimated by those who signed up to go to the new missions.

The viceroy, Antonio de Mendosa, who admired Father Cancer, allotted the missioner a vessel, the caravel *Santa Maria de la Encina*, and appointed Juan de Araña its captain. Father Cancer selected four fellow Dominicans to accompany him — Father Diego de Peñolosa (also known as Diego de Tolosa from the place of his birth), Father Gregory de Beteta, Father John García and a Brother

Father Luís Cancer de Barbastro, martyred in Florida, 1549

Fuentes, a lay Brother about whom few details exist. Early in 1549 the group sailed from Vera Cruz, going first to Cuba to take on supplies. Here, a converted Florida Indian woman, Magdalen, was added to the group as an interpreter.

The original plan was for a landing to be made at Santa Elena Bay on the Atlantic coast of Florida, but for some reason the captain sailed through the Keys and went up the west coast, where the Indians were more hostile because of previous Spanish depredations by De Soto. The captain set as his destination the bay of Espiritu Santo (Tampa Bay). Father Cancer, who was keeping an account for the viceroy, wrote that he was not happy with this decision. (After Cancer's death, Father de Beteta finished the journal and brought it back to Mexico.) There was some difficulty in finding the desired landfall.

On Ascension Day, May 30, 1542, contact was made with Indians, somewhere south of Tampa Bay. Through Magdelen, the missioners learned that the bay they sought was not very far to the north. While the others returned to the *Santa María*, Father Peñalosa, Brother Fuentes, one sailor, and Magdalen remained behind. Father Cancer was apprehensive, but until darkness had fallen no hostile activity could be seen on shore. The next morning, returning ashore, the Spaniards found Magdalen with some Indians, but their Spanish companions were missing. The Indian woman said they had gone to see the chief and that they all would meet at Espiritu Santo.

Reluctantly, Father Cancer decided to go on. The coast was explored, and each time a party of Spaniards landed, Magdalen was there with the Indians to assure them that the Father and Brother were with the chief and would meet them at Espiritu Santo. On June 22 the *Santa María* reached what was believed to be Espiritu Santo. The next day the missioners were ashore. When they returned in the evening to the ships, they found a new Spaniard aboard. He was Juan Muños, who had been captured during the De Soto expedition and held as a slave. When he had learned of the caravel, he stole a canoe and escaped. He told them that the two missioners were dead. They had been tortured "with all kinds of ceremonies and addresses," killed and then scalped. They had been martyred probably on the day after they landed, May 31. The seaman was held as a slave.

With supplies running low, Captain de Araña said that he had had enough. The party would return to Mexico. Father Cancer replied that they had come to convert the Indians and could not return. He asked Juan Muños to remain with him as interpreter, but the former captive wanted no more of the Indians and refused. On June 20, the Feast of Corpus Christi, Mass was celebrated on shore. Then the ship moved south. There was a storm, and rough waters prevented a landing until June 26. Father Cancer spent the time writing letters and bringing his journal up to date. On Wednesday, June 26, the ship stood off the bay of the Caloosahatchie River. It was here that Father Cancer chose to begin his mission. The priests and several oarsmen left the ship in a tender. As they approached the beach, Indians appeared. For some reason, perhaps because he wanted to test the Indians, Father Cancer told his companions to wait offshore. He climbed into the water and waded to land. A crowd of Indians gathered around him, and in view of the two Fathers and sailors he was brutally killed. The Indians shot arrows at the tender, which was forced to retreat to the mother ship. Thus in one account of the martyrdom, Father Cancer "calmly, deliberately, and of his own free choice walked into the very jaws of death for love of his God and neighbor." The great Las Casas called him a saint. The historian John G. Shea wrote: "Thus perished, in obedience to a sense of duty, Father Luís Cancer de Barbastro, one of the most remarkable missionaries of his order, whose wonderful sway over the Indians of Central America justified a confidence that the same means would influence the Mobilian tribes."

Sources:
CCCMUS
Kenny, Michael, S.J., *The Romance of the Floridas*
O'Daniel, V.F., O.P., *Dominicans in Early Florida* (see for original Spanish sources)
Shea, John Gilmary, "History of the Catholic Church Among Indian Tribes," *The Catholic Church of Colonial Days*
Dutto, L.A., "Father Luís [Cancer] de Barbastro," *Ecclesiastical Review*, July and August 1902

Kansas

7. Father Diego de la Cruz, Dominican (1553)
8. Father Hernando Méndez, Dominican (1553)
9. Father Juan Ferrer, Dominican (1553)
10. Brother Juan de Mena, Dominican (1553)

There is some doubt whether these men should be included in a list of American martyrs because their deaths seem not to be as the result of *odium fidei* (hatred of the Faith) but simply because they were in the wrong place at the wrong time. However, as they were included in the list of martyrs prepared by the American bishops for submission to Rome, they are listed here.

In the spring of 1553, a fleet of twenty ships sailed from Vera Cruz for Spain. Among the approximately one thousand passengers were five Dominicans — three priests and two Brothers. Somewhere in the vicinity of Cuba, the vessels were engulfed in a severe tropical depression, possibly a hurricane, and sixteen of the ships were driven back across the Gulf of Mexico and wrecked off the coast of Texas with a great loss of life by drowning and, among the survivors, by starvation.

One of the ships, a galleon, sank off Padre Island. Among the survivors were the five Dominicans, who decided to travel overland to reach Tampico and safety, along with a layman, Francisco Vasquez. Only the Dominican Brother Marcos de Mena and Vasquez reached their goal. They reported that Fathers Diego de la Cruz and Hernando Méndez had been wounded by Indians and died on the banks of the Rio Grande while seeking friendly Indians to whom they could preach the Gospel. Brother Juan de Mena had died near another river farther west, from an arrow that had pierced his back. It was not clear whether Father Juan Ferrer, a relative of St. Vincent Ferrer, died from wounds or exhaustion.

The wreck of the galleon was discovered 600 yards off Padre Island in about 20 feet of water, and over the summers of 1972 and 1973, under the supervision of the Texas Antiquities Committee, some 25,000 pounds of artifacts were recovered, thus concluding the story of the tragedy.

Sources:
CCCMUS
Habig, Marian A., unpublished notes
Southwest Airlines Magazine, July 1974 (reprinted from *Texas Highways*)

Florida

11. Father Pedro Martínez, Jesuit (1566)
Jesuit Protomartyr of the United States

Father Pedro Martínez was born on October 26, 1533, at Teruel in Aragón, where his uncle was regent. He was well educated and, as a layman at the University of Valencia, was known for his brilliance, if not studiousness, and for outstanding swordplay. Eventually, he was drawn to the Jesuits, and on October 2, 1553, was admitted to the Society, in which he became known for his penances and his kindnesses to the dying. He was ordained in 1558, ahead of time, so that he could serve as chaplain in an expedition to Africa against the Moors. When the young priest returned from Africa, St. Francis Borgia wrote to the Jesuit General that "Master Martínez, who is a good theologian and preacher and works with fervor and energy," should be kept in mind for Peru, where the viceroy had asked for some Jesuits.

Father Martínez wrote to the General that his hope was to go to the Indies — East or West — and suffer for Christ. In a later letter he told the General he was ready to endure "toil, hunger, thirst, sleeping on the ground, etc." and added that "the only bodily ache I know is the pain of hair-shirt and scourge. I don't see why God has given me such robustness unless it is to offer it to Him by my service and, if He grants it, with my life. . . . I often dream while I sleep that I am undergoing martyrdom, and, though I know I do not merit it, I long for it above all else and beg first that grace of God."

In the early spring of 1566, the order came for him to leave at once for Seville and the Floridas. On May 31, 1566, he made the solemn profession of four vows to the Society and spent his time preaching and catechizing until the ship sailed. The coast of Florida was reached on August 28, the Feast of St. Augustine, and the ship began searching for the colony of St. Augustine when it was hit by a hurricane and forced out to sea. When the storm passed, the ship returned to the coast again to search for its destination. Water supplies were running low, and a party was sent ashore in a small boat to seek water. Father Martínez went with the group. It was September 14 when the priest first set foot on American shores, on one of Georgia's Golden Isles.

A letter to St. Francis Borgia, the Jesuit Superior General, from one Don Alonzo López of Santo Domingo told what happened next. He had received his information from a survivor of the landing party. While they were ashore, a sudden storm came up, and the mother ship was driven from its mooring, far out to sea. The landing party waited twelve days for it to return. Suffering from hunger but buoyed up by the good spirits of Father Martínez, the men decided to seek the Spanish fort on their own. They rowed to the mainland and explored a river, seeking friendly Indians. Finding no Indian village, they headed south, traveling for three days until they came upon another river. Rowing up the inlet, on the second day they found a small Indian village, whose inhabitants fled. An alligator — "a very large lizard" — was left there roasting. They took half, leaving behind a coat and a glass-beaded necklace as payment.

They returned to their boat, feasted on the meat, and slept in midstream that night. Next morning the Indians, pleased by the payment left behind, appeared on shore. The Indians brought them more food, and Father Martínez gave them some presents. Through signs, the travelers learned that the Spanish fort was three Indian chiefdoms away. They passed through the first chief's area and landed in the second to obtain some fish from Indians. Several Flemish seamen had gone up a hill to the village when Indians came out of the brush and surrounded the boat. The Indians seemed hostile, and Father Martínez told the crew to be ready to leave when the Flemings returned. At that, the Indians seized Father Martínez, a Spanish sailor, and two Flemings and tried to drown them.

Father Martínez was dragged to shore and thrown on the bank. The priest rose to his knees, with a hand grasping the cruxifix he wore. He was struck on the head with a heavy club. "He surely went straight to heaven," continued the report, "where, please God, I hope to meet him again." The Spaniard Flores, who made the report, and three surviving Flemings, though wounded, managed to get the boat away and back to open sea. By sheer chance, they were discovered by a Spanish ship and brought to safety. They learned that the Indians who had killed the priest and three companions had been turned against Spaniards by a Huguenot refugee, a

Pierre Bren. The religious hostilities of Europe had come to the New World. The site of the martyrdom was just north of Jacksonville and the St. John River, near the southern end of Amelia Island. The date of martyrdom was October 6, 1566.

Sources:
CCCMUS
Kenny, Michael, *The Romance of the Floridas*
                    Pedro Martínez, Martyr of Florida
Cicognani, A.G., *Sanctity in America*
See also:
Monumenta Historica Societatis Jesu (Borgia, Spanish Assistency volumes)
Archives of the Indies
See: Bibliography of *Romance of the Floridas*

Virginia

12. Father Luís de Quirós, Jesuit (1571)
13. (Novice) Gabriel de Solís, Jesuit (1571)
14. (Novice) Juan Bautista Méndez, Jesuit (1571)
15. Father Juan Bautista de Segura, Jesuit (1571)
16. (Novice) Christóbal Redondo, Jesuit (1571)
17. Brother Gabriel Gómez, Jesuit (1571)
18. Brother Pedro Linares, Jesuit (1571)
19. Brother Sancho Zeballos, Jesuit (1571)
Protomartyrs of Virginia

Spanish exploration of the Floridas (a term that embraced all the territory north of the Gulf of Mexico) proceeded up the Atlantic coast. A dozen missions had been established above St. Augustine, the northernmost being Santa Elena, south of what is now Charleston, S.C. Spanish ships had entered Chesapeake Bay, and penetration of some of its rivers had been made. An area in what is now northern Virginia was given the name Ajacan, which Kenny thinks might be a corruption of Occoan or Occoquan, place names that remain to this day. The Villafane expedition had brought to Mexico an Indian from the area who had been baptized with the name of his patron, Don Luís Velasco, Governor of Mexico. The Indian went to Spain, where he won the favor of the King and set imaginations aflame with his stories of waterways in his land that could open a sea route to China.

The Spanish King, Philip II, had expressed his desire for the conversion of the people of Ajacan, and an expedition was organized and put in the care of the Jesuits in Havana. Father Juan Bautista de Segura, vice-provincial, was appointed superior for the task. He selected three new missioners who had come from Spain as educators. Father Luís de Quirós, a native of Jerez de la Frontera, had headed a Jesuit college among the Moors of Spain. Brother Gabriel Gómez, also from Andalusia, had taught in a college in Seville and then with Father Quirós. Brother Sancho Zeballos appealed directly to Cuban Governor Pedro Menendez for his New World assignment and was thus included in the party from Spain. To this group was added Brother Pedro Linares and three novices — Gabriel de Solís, Juan Bautista Méndez and Cristóbal Redondo.

Father de Segura had recently returned from a visit to Guale and Santa Elena, the northernmost missions, and he had seen the difficulty in converting Indians when hungry Spanish soldiers raided their stores. He decided that no Spanish soldiers would be taken along to give bad example; instead they would take the Indian Don Luís, who was the brother of the chief of Ajacan and whose help would be more valuable than any soldiers. Supplies and Mass necessities were put aboard the mission vessel, and the group sailed to Santa Elena. Here a boy, Alonso Olmos, called by the diminutive Aloncito, was added to the group. The boy was the son of a settler at Santa Elena, where he served Mass for the Franciscan Father. He begged to be allowed to go with them to perform the same service. He would be the only one to survive.

The vessel carrying the missioners reached the Chesapeake (St. Mary's Bay) in early September. They proceeded up the bay and into the Potomac, which they followed for twenty leagues (sixty miles), and then entered a freshwater stream for three more leagues. Here they made their first camp and landed their belongings. The ship left for Havana on September 12, 1570, carrying a letter from Father Quirós reporting that the country was in the midst of famine, with even roots and berries failing. Father de Segura sent an urgent plea for supplies, particularly seed corn to help the Indians plant. The priest said that he was locating the mission along a stream two leagues up river.

Within two days Don Luís excused himself to go and see his brother. The missioners thought nothing of it and began getting their settlement ready. They built a residential cabin and a chapel. The baptism of a dying child gave them their first native Christian. Then reports begin to filter in that Don Luís had returned to native ways and was leading a life of unbridled vice. Father de Segura attempted to get him to return but without avail. The winter was very hard, for their poorly constructed cabin gave little protection from the cold. Supplies ran out, and they hunted for herbs, roots, and berries to remain alive. Because they were without protection, Father de Segura led them in daily spiritual exercises to keep them ready for whatever might come.

In February 1571, Father de Segura dispatched Father Quirós to attempt again to persuade Luís to return. He also asked him to try getting some mats as protection from the cold. He sent two novices, Gabriel de Solís and Juan Bautista Méndez, as companions and to help carry the mats. The Jesuits found Luís, but the reception was hostile. Father Quirós began to exhort Luís to return to Christian ways, but the answer was a sign from the renegade and a flight of arrows from his Algonquin cohorts. Then the Indians fell on the Spaniards with tomahawks and clubs. Father Quirós and Gabriel de Solís were killed on the spot. Novice Méndez, wounded, was able to escape into the woods. The Indians found his body the next morning where he had died from his wounds. The date of the massacre was February 4, 1571. The Indians burned all the bodies to ashes.

Five days later, Luís and a party of Indians came to St. Mary's Mission, as the Jesuits had named their settlement. As a letter in Jesuit archives recounts it, "Don Luís, garbed in the clothing he had stripped from the corpse of Father Quirós, entered the house with a few picked braves armed with axes and machetes he had borrowed, and he assigned a part to each warrior so that all the missioners might fall in the first onslaught and none could go to the assistance of another. When Father de Segura, wholly unsuspecting, saw Don Luís enter, he greeted him very cordially and bade him welcome. Before he could get further, Don Luís answered with a blow from a borrowed ax that he carried and rained blow after blow on the missioner's arms and legs and whole body, leaving it covered with gaping wounds. Thus did he repay the innumerable kindnesses that holy priest had showered on him. While their leader was thus showing his gratitude to his benefactor, the others, like ravenous wolves, fell on those gentle lambs who did harm to none and good to all. They entered the kitchen and found Brother Cristóbal Redondo, who, in body and soul and disposition and voice, was an angel rather than a human being. Seeing those wild beasts and bleeding from the wounds, he cried out for help; but it was too late to seek aid from his brethren. Brothers Gómez and Linares had already fallen victims, and having met Brother Sancho Zaballos, who had gone out with Alonso for firewood, [the Indians] cleft his head open with an ax."

Alonso begged to be killed with his friends, but Luís said

he was too young and that it was only the missioners he wanted to destroy. The boy did persuade Luís to give the missioners decent burial, each with a crucifix in his hand. The date of the martyrdom was February 9, 1571. Alonso was rescued the following year by Governor Menendez, and it was he who told the sad story of the massacre. The grave of St. Mary's was never found, although with the crucifixes it should be identifiable if discovered. But then, even the site of the mission is not known today.

Sources:
CCCMUS
Nevins, Albert J., *Our American Catholic Heritage*, "The Colony That Failed"
Kenny, Michael, *The Romance of the Floridas*
                      The Martyrs of Virginia
Cicognani, A. G., *Sanctity in America*

New Mexico

20. Father Juan de Santa María, Franciscan (1581)
21. Father Francisco López, Franciscan (1582)
22. Brother Augustín Rodríguez, Franciscan (1582)

These three Franciscan missioners, together with some soldiers and Indians, left Chihuahua, Mexico, June 5, 1581, to survey the tribes of New Mexico for missionary work. Father López was the superior of the group. They visited a number of pueblos and realized that New Mexico represented a large and promising field for conversions. While at the Tano pueblo of Galisteo, Father López decided to send Father de Santa María back to Mexico for more missioners. On the third day out, September 10, 1581, near Chilili, Father de Santa María was waylaid by a roving band of Tigua Indians and killed. The murderers burned his body.

Father Francisco and Brother Augustín went to Tiguex, the old Coronado base, and there set up their mission. The soldiers were sent back to Mexico. In May of 1582, while praying, Father López was attacked by a Tigua Indian and killed by two blows to the head. Brother Augustín buried his superior's body and then went to the pueblo of Santiago, farther up the Rio Grande River, thinking it a safer place. However, he too was killed and his body thrown into the Rio Grande when it was in flood. According to the chronicles of José Arlegui, the Christian converts of the missioners were also put to death. These martyrdoms were brought about by the enmity of pueblo medicine men who saw the priests as a threat to their own positions.

Father Gerónimo de Zarate Salmerón wrote a history of these missions (1538-1626) in 1629. He relates that, thirty-three years after the murder of Father López, a Tigua Indian who had seen the killing showed a friar the grave. The body was exhumed, and the skull bore witness of the two fatal blows. The body was taken to the church in Sandia and there interred. Father Salmerón concluded that the blood of martyrs is truly the seed of Christianity, for the mission in 1629 had almost thirty-five thousand Christian baptisms recorded, and the Indians were served from forty-three churches and chapels.

Sources:
CCCMUS
Habig, Marion A., *Heroes of the Cross*

23. Father Pedro de Corpa, Franciscan (1597)
24. Father Blas de Rodríguez, Franciscan (1597)
25. Father Miguel de Auñón, Franciscan (1597)
26. Brother Antonio de Badajoz, Franciscan (1597)
27. Father Francisco Verascola, Franciscan (1597)
Protomartyrs of Georgia

The Spanish missioners moving north from St. Augustine established missions on what are called the Golden Islands of Georgia — Cumberland, Jekyll, St. Simon's, and others — together with missions on the mainland, to Christianize the Guale Indians. This work was begun in 1587, and the pioneer missioners were Father Pedro de Corpa, from Castile, who established a mission at Tolomato, opposite Sapelo Island; Father Blas de Rodríguez, from San Gabriel Province, Spain, who staffed Tupiqui, opposite St. Catherine's Island; and Brother Antonio de Badajoz, older than the others, also from San Gabriel. In 1595 three more priests arrived. Father Miguel de Auñón, a native of Zaragoza, Spain, "of a well-known family, of noble blood, a man of great spirit, grace, and voice, loved and cherished by all," was assigned to open a mission on Guale Island, the northernmost mission, which he named St. Catherine of Guale (St. Catherine's Island). Because Father did not know the language, Brother Antonio was sent to assist him and act as translator. Father Francisco de Verascola, called the "Calabrian Giant" because of his huge size, a native of Vizcaya, Spain, established the Misión Santo Domingo on St. Simon Island. The last of the newcomers was Father Francisco de Avila, from Toledo, who founded Misión San Buenaventura (Asao) on Jekyll Island.

Each mission became a center of Catholic life, with the Christian converts moving from their own villages to live around the mission. These missions established patterns

35

that would be followed later by Father Serra in California. All was proceeding serenely in the Georgia mission until September 1597. Juanillo, the Christian son of a chief, decided to take a second wife. Father de Corpa told the young man that he could not do this, as it was against the teaching of the Church. When Juanillo refused to listen to the priest, Father de Corpa denounced him publicly. Enraged, Juanillo left the village, went into the forest, and gathered some pagan Indians. On the eve of September 13, the renegade and his followers returned to the village, their bodies smeared in red paint, with feathers in their hair — a sign that they were making war. The next morning they broke into the mission and found Father Pedro at prayer. He was dispatched with a blow of a tomahawk to his head. The Indians severed the priest's head and set it up on a pole at the landing place as a warning to others. The body of the slain Franciscan was dragged into the woods and buried secretly so that Christians would not find it. Other Indians raped Christian women, and the mission itself was looted.

While a messenger was sent to St. Catherine's Island to ask the chief there to kill Father de Auñón and Brother Antonio (which he refused to do, although he did warn the Brother of the danger), the band under Juanillo went to Tupique, about ten miles north, and broke in on Father Blas, saying they were going to kill him. The priest asked to be allowed to say Mass, and for some reason his request was granted. He gave to the Christian women of the mission what little personal possessions he had. For two more days they held the Spaniard prisoner. During this time, Ore says, "he prepared for death with the best disposition and care he could, like a good religious and Christian." On September 17 he too was murdered by a blow to the head. The rebellious Indians threw the body out to be eaten by dogs. An old man, a Christian, took the body secretly and buried it in the woods. Because the old man died before friars returned, the burial place is unknown.

The Indians then set out for St. Catherine Island, where Father Auñón and Brother Antonio resided. The chief who had warned the Brother again advised the Brother and Father Commissary to escape, and he offered a canoe and rowers to take them to San Pedro Mission on Cumberland Island. Brother Antonio, who did not take the warning seriously because he knew nothing of what had happened on the mainland, again dismissed the advice. By this time the rebel Indians had reached the mission. Brother Antonio was killed first by a blow to his head. The renegade Christians drew back from Father de Auñón because he was held in great respect, but a pagan Indian rendered him unconscious with a tomahawk. Some of the Christian Indians gathered about the fallen man to defend him, but a second pagan Indian struck a blow which smashed the head open. When the murderers retreated, the Christians took both bodies and buried them at the foot of a large cross Father de Auñón had erected. Here they were recovered six years later when the mission was reopened.

Two missioners were still alive. Father de Verascola had gone to the mission center at St. Augustine to bring back supplies and was thus away when the massacres took place. He was in charge of St. Dominic's Mission on Asao (St. Simon's Island). He returned, totally unaware of the tragedy that had befallen his fellow workers. When he stepped ashore, two Indians seized him while another murdered him with an ax. He died sometime in the latter part of September and was buried at the mission.

This murder left only Father Francisco de Avila alive. He had received word of the uprising and hid when the renegades came for him. While the Indians were looting the mission, he escaped into the woods, but he was spotted and wounded by arrows. Taken prisoner, he was at first condemned to die until it was decided to keep him alive as a slave. He became servant to all, abused by his captors and jeered at by the children. The Indians tried to make him give up his religion, get married, and serve in a spirit house. He resisted and after nine months of enslavement was rescued by Spanish troops. Taken to St. Augustine, he was asked to testify against the murderers, but he claimed clerical immunity, saying he could not give evidence that would lead to the deaths of others. He went to Havana and under obedience wrote out all he knew of the affair, and this document was heavily used by Father Luís Gerónimo de Ore in his "Relación de los Mártires." Father Avila returned to Spain, where he died.

Sources:
CCCMUS
Franciscan Studies, "Missions and Martyrs of Spanish Florida" (June 1941).
Geiger, Maynard, *Franciscan Conquest of Florida*
  Biographical Dictionary
de Ore, Luís Gerónimo, *Relación de los Mártires*
Habig, Marion, "The Five Martyrs of Guale," *Franciscan Herald*

New Mexico

28. Father Pedro de Ortega, O.F.M. (1631)

The American bishops' list of martyrs includes the name of Father Pedro de Ortega, and the inclusion is based on a report made in 1635 by a Father Ocaña, who said that the priest was poisoned by Jumanos Indians. Although New Mexico is assigned to this martyr, there is a possibility that the death took place in Texas. (Source: Lemmens, *Geschichte Franziskanermissionem*, p. 235.) There was a Father Juan Ortega who worked among the Jumanos in Texas for a period of six months, but he was not a martyr (Castaneda I, pp. 203-204).

New Mexico

29. Father Pedro Miranda, O.F.M. (1631)

As in Georgia, many Indians of Taos pueblo resented the Christian teaching of monogamous marriage. The unrest caused by this doctrine is believed to underlie the attack made at the Taos mission on December 28, 1631. Because of the cold, two Spanish guards, Luís Pacheco and Juan de Estrada, had gone to the mission kitchen to warm themselves. While they were there, a mob of Indians, instigated by medicine men, broke into the mission and killed the guards. The Indians found Father Miranda at prayer and murdered him.

Sources:
CCCMUS
Habig, Marion, *Heroes of the Cross*

New Mexico

30. Father Francisco Letrado, O.F.M. (1632)

One of the famous landmarks of the Southwest is Inscription Rock (*El Morro*). It was a guidepost for wagon trains going west, and film director John Ford featured it prominently in several of his western movies. Early travelers carved names, dates, and destinations into the face of the rock to let others know they had at least reached this point. One of the earliest inscriptions was carved in Spanish by a soldier named Lujan. Translated, this message reads: "They passed on March 23, 1632, to avenge the death of Father

Letrado. Lujan." The reference was to an expedition sent out by the governor of New Mexico, Francisco de la Mora Ceballos, to punish those Zuni Indians who had killed Father Francisco Letrado, and it was signed by a member of the troop.

Father Francisco Letrado was the pastor of the mission at Hawikuh (Aguico), near Zuni, New Mexico. Toward the third week in February 1632, he was visited by a fellow Franciscan, Father Martín de Arvide, who was on his way to establish a mission among the Moqui (Hopi) Indians. Accompanying Father de Arvide were two soldiers, Bartolomé de Amihbia, a Spaniard, and Roque García, a Mexican, plus a mestizo youth, Lorenzo, whom Father de Arvide had raised from a child. The two missioners had much to talk over and probably used the occasion for each to receive the Sacrament of Penance. Father Letrado told his friend of the difficulties of his work, caused by the opposition of pagan medicine men who saw the priest as a threat to their own power. After the visit, enjoyed by both men, Father de Arvide and his companions left to continue their journey.

A few days later it was a Sunday, and when no one showed up for Mass, Father Letrado went into the pueblo to find out what was wrong. He met some pagans, and seeing that they were intent on doing him harm, he knelt down, took his crucifix into his hands, and commended his soul to God. An Indian killed him with an arrow. He was scalped, and the Indians used the trophy in a pagan dance. The date of the martyrdom was February 22. The soldiers who arrived later never found the missioner's body.

Sources:
CCCMUS
Habig, Marion, *Heroes of the Cross*

31. Father Martín de Arvide, Franciscan (1632)
Protomartyr of Arizona

After Father Letrado had been killed, his murderers went in pursuit of his visitor, Father Martín de Arvide, who was headed for the Moqui (Hopi) Indians in Arizona, where other missioners were at work, a distance of about seven days from Hawikuh. Some old manuscripts refer to the tribe as Zipia, and this is assumed to be the Zuni name for the Moqui, who dwelt to the west of the Zuni.

Father de Arvide had been traveling for five or six days when the pursuers caught up with his party on February 27. The two soldiers were put to death first, and then the Franciscan was beaten with clubs. The youth Lorenzo, who had been raised by the missioner, became an apostate, probably to save himself. He hacked off the priest's right hand and then his scalp while the priest was still alive. These further indignities caused the missioner's death.

Sources:
CCCMUS
Habig, Marion, *Heroes of the Cross*

32. Father Francisco Porras, Franciscan (1633)

Between the years 1935 and 1939, an archaeological team from Harvard University excavated the site of the Moqui (Hopi) Indian village of Awatovi (Awatobi) in northern Arizona. Among other findings, they uncovered the foundations of a large church and in its ruins found the grave of a Franciscan missionary, possibly the founder of the parish, Father Francisco Porras.

Father Porras arrived among the Moquis in 1629 to found Misión San Bernardo at Awatovi. He was accompanied by two other Franciscans, who were put in charge of Moqui outstations. Father Porras, while studying the Hopi language, began the building of the church that would be the center of their work. Within nine months he had mastered the Indian tongue, and his work was blessed with success, particularly after treating and restoring sight to the chief's twelve-year-old son, who had been blind from birth. He was baptizing about a thousand Indian converts a year.

However, his success brought the enmity of tribal medicine men, who managed to poison his food. Shortly after eating the food, Father Porras realized what had happened. He sent for one of his companions, from whom he received the last sacraments on his knees. He began to recite Psalm 31, "In you, O Lord, I take refuge." When he reached the verse, "Into your hands I commend my spirit," he expired.

Sources:
CCCMUS
Habig, Marion, unpublished notes

New Mexico

33. Father Diego de San Lucas, Franciscan (1639)

Father Diego de San Lucas arrived in Mexico from Spain in 1628 and was assigned to work among the pueblo Indians of New Mexico. In 1639, when he was guardian of one of the Jemez missions, he was shot to death by arrows, possibly during an Apache raid. He may have been guardian to San Diego Church in Jemez pueblo, but the circumstances of his martyrdom are not clear.

Sources:
CCCMUS
Habig, Marion, unpublished notes

New York

34. St. René Goupil, Layman (1642)
Protomartyr of New York

While there may be a tendency to regard the Catholic lay missioner as a product of our own times, devoted laymen were used by the French in establishing the Faith in North America. St. René Goupil, the protomartyr of New York State, was such a person.

René Goupil was born in Anjou, France, in 1606. He joined the Jesuits but had to leave the Society because of ill health. Still dedicated to a life of service, he undertook the study of medicine and became a surgeon. In 1638 he went to New France (Canada) to use his skills in the mission work that the Church was conducting there. He worked in a hospital in Quebec and in 1640 became a *donné* (lay missioner) to serve the Huron Indians. In June of 1642, Father Isaac Jogues, S.J., came to Quebec gathering supplies for a mission he was to begin in Georgian Bay. Father Jogues enlisted the aid of Goupil, and the two men went to Three Rivers to complete preparations for the journey west.

There final preparations were made and Father Jogues enlisted another lay missioner. William Couture, to join the party. On August 1 the expedition set out on the St. Lawrence, despite rumors that maurauding Mohawks had been seen in the area through which they would have to pass. The party consisted of the three Frenchmen plus Teresa, a Christian Huron girl, and about forty Huron braves who were returning home. With twelve canoes carrying all these people, Father Jogues felt that they were safe from attack.

The first day on the river passed without incident, although, unknown to the missioners, they were being stalked by Mohawks. On the second day, shortly after dawn as the party started out anew, the trap was sprung. Mohawk canoes suddenly appeared. The seven rear canoes escaped, but the forward five with the Frenchmen and the girl were cut off. An order was given to beach the canoes and flee into the forest. Jogues, Couture and Teresa escaped into the woods. From his place of concealment, Jogues saw that Goupil had been captured. Then Teresa was found and dragged from the forest. Jogues realized that he could not allow his charges to be taken into captivity and possible death alone, so he surrendered himself. Couture was also brought in.

The Mohawks and their captives began the journey south to their villages. It took five days to reach Lake Champlain, where the raiders joined a larger band of Mohawks. The captives were forced to run the gauntlet and were beaten and branded. The war party set out again and after many days reached the Mohawk center of Ossernenon, now called Auriesville, which was located on the Mohawk River, west of Fort Orange (Albany). The Indian village was at the top of a hill, and the prisoners had to run another gauntlet uphill while women beat them with clubs and sticks. The Frenchmen were tied to posts and tortured. Women chewed Jogues' fingers, and the priest and Goupil each had a thumb cut off. The prisoners were then divided among various villages, with Jogues and Goupil kept as slaves at Ossernenon.

The days that followed were difficult. The two Frenchmen had to do women's work, laboring in the fields and hauling water and firewood. They were given only leavings of food. On September 29, 1642, Goupil instinctively made the Sign of the Cross over a sick child. Two young braves saw him. Realizing that he was in trouble, Goupil went to a ravine behind the village, where Father Jogues had gone to pray. He told the missioner what he had done. The two missioners began to recite the Rosary. The two braves stepped into the clearing. One forced Goupil to his knees while the other smashed in Goupil's skull with a tomahawk, as Father Jogues gave absolution. Then the priest was ordered back to the village.

The next day Father Jogues went looking for the body of his companion. He found it thrown on a garbage heap. He hid it under the bank of a stream that ran through the ravine, until he might have the opportunity to bury it. When he returned the next day, the body was gone. He could never find it. He did not know whether it had been washed away, dragged off by an animal, or hidden by the Indians. Goupil was included in the list of eight North American martyrs canonized by Pope Pius XI on October 19, 1930. Their feast is celebrated on September 26.

Sources:

Cicognani, A. G., *Sanctity in America*
Nevins, Albert J., *Builders of Catholic America*
Delaney, John, *Dictionary of Saints*
Wynne, John J., *The Jesuit Martyrs of North America*
Talbot, Francis, *Saint Among Savages*

New York

35. St. Isaac Jogues, Jesuit (1646)
36. St. John de Lalande, Layman (1646)
(See preceding sketch: St. René Goupil)

After René Goupil was murdered, Father Jogues was transferred from the longhouse where he had been living to the supervision of an elderly woman who was held in high regard by the Iroquois. She was the mother of a chief and had been a daughter and wife of chiefs. She treated the cap-

Saint Isaac Jogues, martyred in New York, 1646

tive with kindness, giving him a copy of *The Imitation of Christ* which had been among the booty captured. Father Jogues called her "aunt," and she referred to him as "nephew." It was still a considerable comedown for one who had been part of a well-to-do French family.

Father Isaac Jogues was born in Orleans on January 10, 1607. He attended a Jesuit school and admired his black-robed teachers. When he was seventeen, he was admitted to the Jesuits, despite parental objections. He was ordained in January 1636 and left in April of that year for New France. After a short stay in Quebec he moved to the Jesuit center in Three Rivers. He learned the Huron language, preached, converted and baptized. He made two long mission journeys, the first to the Niagara River, near the present site of Buffalo, and the second to the French outpost of Sault Ste. Marie. In 1642 he was assigned to the Huron mission of Ihonatiria on Georgian Bay. It was while setting off for this mission with René Goupil that he was captured by the Mohawks.

Father Jogues's Indian guardian allowed him considerable liberty. He went on hunting and fishing parties, and it was during one of these outings that he seized the opportunity to escape. The Indians had taken him to the Hudson River, south of Fort Orange, perhaps to the Catskill Creek, where fish spawned. On their return journey they stayed in the barn of a Dutch settler who was married to a Mohawk woman. During the night, while his captors slept, Father Jogues slipped away and went to Fort Orange. The Dutch settlers hid him until the angry search for the fugitive died down. Then they smuggled him aboard a ship bound for Nieuw Amsterdam (New York), where in November he boarded a ship for Europe, landing Christmas Day on the Breton Coast. His return to France was something of a sensation, since it was presumed that he was dead. His mangled hands were an object of curiosity to the French and of anguish to himself, since by Church law the amputation prevented him from saying Mass. The Queen of France petitioned the Pope on his behalf, and the answer came: "It would be shameful that a martyr of Christ not be permitted to drink the blood of Christ."

Thus restored to the altar, Father Jogues asked his superiors to send him back to New France. There was a reluctance on their part because of concern for his safety and the fact that he so well represented the Society in France. However, Jogues's desire won the day, and in the spring of 1644 he sailed again to Canada, taking up residence in Montréal. The new French governor, Charles de Montmagny, who had been on the ship with Jogues, sent out peace feelers to the Mohawks, and in late summer Indian and French delegations met as an uneasy truce began to take form. The governor promised that when spring came he would send an ambassador to the Mohawks for finalization of the peace.

Father Jogues was the governor's choice to represent France. The Jesuit knew the language, the customs, and the people. In May of 1646 Jogues set out for Iroquois land. He was accompanied by Jean Bordon, a French cartographer, two Algonquin ambassadors, and a Mohawk escort. He took with him a box of Mass necessities, which he was to leave with Aunt. After passing through Lake Champlain, the party entered another lake that was on no French map. Bordon sketched it on his drawing, and Jogues named the discovery "Lake of the Blessed Sacrament." Later the English changed the name to Lake George in honor of their own king. The party made a stop at Fort Orange, where Jogues thanked those who had aided in his escape. Jogues met the Iroquois council near Ossernenon (where he had left his box), and the peace treaty that had been worked out in Montréal was accepted. However, the chiefs announced it was only between the French and the Christian Hurons and Algonquins. He learned that two of the Iroquois tribes, the Senecas and Oneidas, had sent war parties against non-Christian Hurons. He realized that these warriors would not be able to distinguish a Christian from a pagan and that the treaty was thus flawed. He decided to return immediately and report his finding to the governor.

Father Jogues met with Montmagny and told him that even if the Iroquois could distinguish Christian Indians, the pagans would believe the French had sold them out and mission work among them would be destroyed. The governor decided to send a delegation of Hurons to work the matter out. Jogues said he would go with them, not as an ambassador but as a missioner who would remain among the Mohawks. The party consisted of Father Jogues, Otrihoure, the Huron ambassador, two Huron braves, who were to desert out of fear, and John de Lalande, a young French *donné*, who was to remain as an assistant to Father Jogues. Lalande had been born in Dieppe, France, and had gone to Quebec to work. There he had joined the Jesuits as a lay missioner.

After twenty days of paddling, portages, and hiking, the party was almost within sight of Ossernenon when a screaming band of Mohawks surrounded them and took them prisoner. Reaching Ossernenon, Jogues was allowed to go to Aunt's house. She told him that the summer had been one of drought and failure of crops, which the medicine men blamed on his box. They had thrown it in the river. Jogues, Lalande and the Huron were allowed to spend the night in Aunt's cabin. The next day the Ossernenon leaders left for a council in a neighboring village to decide what should be done about the prisoners.

While the chiefs were gone, some young braves decided that they would not wait. Jogues was called outside Aunt's house, and when he stepped through the doorway he was struck with a tomahawk blow that killed him. The braves decapitated the body and hung his head on a stake of the palisade surrounding the village. The priest's body was dragged through the village by boys while others kicked it. When the boys tired of their play, they rolled the body down the hill into the Mohawk River. The next day John de Lalande went looking for the body to bury it, but he was intercepted by the same braves and he too was tomahawked. His head joined that of Father Jogues on the palisade. Otrihoure was to die some days later. Father Jogues was martyred on October 18, 1646, and John de Lalande on October 19. Both men were among the eight North American martyrs canonized by Pope Pius XI in 1930. Jogues's death ended all attempts at peace, and Iroquois raids were to bring death to other missioners and decimate the Huron and Algonquin tribes. The Iroquois met their own downfall when they sided with the British in the Revolutionary War.

Sources:
Nevins, Albert J., *Our American Catholic Heritage*
                            Builders of Catholic America
Talbot, Francis, *Saint Among Savages*
The Jesuit Relations
Cigognani, A. G., *Sanctity in America*
Delaney, John, *Dictionary of Saints*
Wynne, John J., *The Jesuit Martyrs of North America*

Florida

37, 38, 39. Three Unnamed Franciscans (1647)

Consulting documents in the General Archives of the Indies, Father Habig, in his *Heroes of the Cross*, writes of three unnamed Franciscans who were put to death by the Apalache Indians in 1647. These unknown martyrs are also included in the list prepared by the American bishops and submitted to Rome.

Habig writes: "The protomartyrs of the Franciscans in Florida, so far as we have been able to ascertain, met their death in 1647. Provoked by the unreasonable demands of

50

the Governor of Spanish Florida, the Indians of the Apalache district rose in rebellion and killed three of the eight missionaries laboring among them, as well as nine other Spaniards. The latter seem to have been the Lieutenant Governor and his family. The documents consulted all state that three missionaries were put to death, but none mentions their names. Hence beyond the fact of their martyrdom we can furnish little information."

The Apalache Indians were centered around the present Tallahassee, and it was in that area the missioners were put to death. As in New Mexico, when Indians revolted against Spanish treatment, they also rose against the religion of the Spaniards, even though the missioners sought their temporal, as well as spiritual, welfare.

Sources:
CCCMUS
Habig, Marion, *Heroes of the Cross*

New Mexico

40. Father Pedro Avila y Ayala, Franciscan (1672)

Father Avila y Ayala was stoned to death by Navajo Indians at Hawikuh, a Zuni pueblo, on October 7, 1672, during a surprise raid. Although the attack was against the Zuni, the missioner was probably killed because he was serving the Navajos' enemies and because of their hatred for Christianity. On the day following the attack, Father Juan Galdo, a Franciscan missioner stationed at a nearby pueblo (Halona), went to Hawikuh and transferred the body of the slain priest to Halona for burial.

Sources: CCCMUS
Habig, Marion, *Heroes of the Cross*

41. Father Alonso Gil de Avila, Franciscan (1675)

The Apache Indians were enemies of the pueblo people and the Spaniards. They made frequent raids on pueblo villages. On January 23, 1675, these feared warriors made a raid on the Piros pueblo of Senecu, during the course of which they killed the mission pastor, Father Alonso Gil de Avila. As a result of the raid, the pueblo was abandoned and the survivors fled to Socorro. Father Gil de Avila's death was reported by Father Nicholas López, superior of the New Mexico missions at the time, but further details are lacking.

Sources:
CCCMUS
Habig, Marion, *Heroes of the Cross*

Martyrs of the 1680 Pueblo Revolt

The Pueblo Revolt, which took place on August 10-11, 1680, in New Mexico and Arizona, took the lives of 21 Franciscans and one Indian who are listed as martyrs in the list submitted to the Holy See by the American bishops; it also brought death to 380 Spanish men, women and children, including some servants. Although the purpose of the revolt was to wipe out both the Church and Spanish rule, some missioners escaped, along with some 1,500 Spaniards.

New Mexico and Arizona counted two types of Indians. There were those who led a nomadic or semi-nomadic life — the Apaches, Navajos and Mansos. Because these tribes were scattered and sparse, mission work among them was difficult. These tribes, particularly the Apache, were raiders and warriors. The second group of southwestern Indians were the pueblo Indians, who dwelt in fixed villages, generation after generation. Most of these people lived in a circle around Santa Fe. These tribes included the Tanos, Tewas, Tiguas and Piros. The Queres Indians lived at Acoma and in its vicinity. The Hopis, also pueblo people, dwelt in northern Arizona, across the border from New Mexico. Because the pueblo people lived in one place, they were agricultural and settled, and were a fertile field for missionary work. The Franciscan padres made large numbers of converts, much to the anger of tribal medicine men whose powers and control were being diminished. While many of these converts were fervent Christians who gave up the old ways, some of them adopted a superficial Christianity, clinging to ancient superstitions and living in fright of the medicine men.

The Spanish authorities, who wanted no dual loyalty, realized that their main opponents were not the chiefs but the medicine men. In an effort to break the hold of these wizards on their villages, the Spanish governor in 1675 arrested forty-seven medicine men, who were convicted of sorcery and witchcraft and confined to a prison in the capital, Santa Fe. Three, however, were hanged as an example. The hangings and imprisonment upset the pagan Indians, and a delegation from Tewa pueblos went to Santa Fe to petition their release. The governor relented and released some medicine men, among them an Indian called Pope, a medicine man from the Tewa pueblo of San Juan. Once back in his village, Pope began planning for an uprising and when he heard that he was to be arrested again, he fled to Taos. There he gathered other dissidents from various pueblos and continued his plans. He contacted other pueblos and even enlisted the Apaches. The uprising was to take place simultaneously in all the peublos on a day chosen by Pope. All the missioners were to be killed and their churches destroyed. All the other Spaniards in and around the pueblos were to be massacred, and the Indians were to return to their native religion.

Not all Indians wanted to participate. Pope warned that any pueblo that did not join the rebellion would be destroyed. He killed his own son-in-law, the Indian governor of San Juan, because he did not trust him to keep the secret. Nevertheless, the Spanish governor in Sante Fe learned on August 9 from loyal Tanos chiefs that the rebellion was to take place on August 11. Pope, hearing that his plot had been exposed, sent out runners, ordering the uprising for August 10. As the account of the American bishops relates it: "From the northern Tigua pueblo of Taos to the southern Tigua pueblo of Isleta (which pueblo, however, did not take part in the revolt), a distance of more than fifty leagues, the whole country except Santa Fe was devastated and depopulated on that single day, August 10, 1680." The martyrs of that insurrection follow.

New Mexico

42. Bartolomé Naranjo, Indian Layman

It is an oddity of the revolt of the Pueblo Indians that the first victim of the uprising should be a Queres Indian, Bartolomé Naranjo, who was killed on the eve of the general massacre, August 9, 1680, in the Queres pueblo of San Felipe on the Rio Grande. Bartolomé lived with his brothers, Francisco Lorenzo and Juan, on a ranch outside San Felipe. The latter brothers went into the pueblo on August 9 and were made prisoners. Near evening prayer time, Bartolomé went into the pueblo and was halted by a group of conspirators, who asked if he was with them and prepared to help kill the Spanish priests. Bartolomé replied that they were crazy and that he would not join them "because it is not right." He was killed on the spot. In the investigation made after the uprising had been put down, the surviving brothers testified to Bartolomé's death.

43. Father Juan Bernal, Franciscan
44. Father Domingo de Vera, Franciscan
45. Father Fernando de Velasco, Franciscan
46. Father Manuel Tinoco, Franciscan

With the exception of the Indian Bartolomé Narajo, who died on the preceding evening, there is no way to determine the order of death of those who perished on August 10, 1680. Father Juan Bernal was the Custos, or superior, of the New Mexico Province. He was a native of Mexico City and had arrived to take up his duties in 1677. He was killed at the Santa Cruz Friary in the pueblo of Galisteo. Murdered with him was Father Domingo de Vera, also a native of Mexico City, who had been working in New Mexico since 1674.

Killed in the vicinity of Galisteo were the other two Franciscans. Father Fernando de Velasco, a native of Cádiz, Spain, was an older man and a veteran missioner, having arrived from Spain thirty years earlier. He was the pastor of the Portiuncula parish in the pueblo of Pecos. Having learned of the planned uprising, he had set out for the mission center at Galisteo to see Father Bernal. On the way he was joined by Father Manuel Tinoco from the pueblo San Marcos, who was on a similar errand to warn their superior. Father Tinoco had arrived in the mission in 1674 from Estremadura, Spain. According to the testimony of Pedro García, an Indian who escaped capture, these latter two missioners were apprehended within sight of Galisteo. Their rosaries were taken from their habits and burned, after which they were put to death. The murderers of these four priests were Tanos Indians.

47. Father Juan Bautista Pío, Franciscan

Although it cannot be said with certainty, it is believed that Father Pío was the first priest killed in the revolt. Father Pío was from Vitoria in the Cantábrica mountains of Spain, and had arrived as a missioner in 1677. He was stationed in Santa Fe, but early on the morning of August 10 he had left his friary to go to Tesuque to say Mass for the feast of St. Lawrence, Martyr, accompanied by a soldier, Pedro Hidalgo. Unknown to him, Tewa Indians at Tesuque were the instigators of the premature revolt. Learning that the plot had been discovered by the Spanish, it was the Tesuque Tewas who decided to advance the date to August 10. They had sent out runners the previous day to tell the other pueblos to begin the revolt on the morrow before the Spanish had time to act.

Father Pío arrived at Tesuque to find the pueblo deserted. He went seeking the Indians and came upon a band of them in a ravine, some armed and in war paint. He tried to get them to come back to the Church, telling them they were foolish to make trouble. He told them that he would help them in their difficulties. The Indians fell upon him and killed him in a bloody manner. Pedro Hidalgo managed to escape, and his later testimony told of the manner of death for Father Pío.

48. Father Tomás de Torres, Franciscan

Father Tomás de Torres was a native Mexican from Teposatlan who went to New Mexico in 1677. He was the pastor of the parish of San Francisco in the Tewa pueblo of Nambe. He was murdered in his friary.

49. Father Antonio de Mora, Franciscan
50. Brother Juan de la Pedrosa, Franciscan

It was in Taos, a Tigua pueblo to which the medicine man Pope had fled, that the plans for the revolt were finalized. This pueblo had already witnessed the martyrdom of Father Pedro Miranda in 1631. Almost fifty years later, two more Franciscans were to die there. The pastor of St. Jerónimo Parish was Father Antonio de Mora, a native of Michoacan, Mexico, who had been working in New Mexico since 1671. He was assisted by Brother Juan de la Pedrosa, a native of Mexico City who had arrived in New Mexico in 1671. These two men were put to death by Tiguas, and their church was desecrated.

51. Father Matías Rendón, Franciscan

Father Rendón died in the Tigua pueblo of Picuris, near Taos. He had arrived in the province in 1674 and came from Los Angeles in Michoacan, Mexico. No witnesses testified as to the manner of his death.

52. Father Luís de Morales, Franciscan
53. Brother Antonio Sánchez de Pro, Franciscan

These two Franciscans were killed at San Ildefonso, a Tewa pueblo on the west bank of the Rio Grande, near Santa Cruz. Father Morales had been a missioner in New Mexico since 1664 and was a native Mexican from Baeza. Brother Sánchez was also from Mexico (San Diego) and had been working in the Santa Fe region since 1677.

New Mexico

54. Father Francisco de Lorenzana, Franciscan
55. Father Juan de Talbán, Franciscan
56. Father José de Montesdoca, Franciscan

Father Francisco Ayeta, a Franciscan missioner of Santa Fe, was in Mexico obtaining supplies when the insurrection broke out. When he returned to New Mexico and found the devastation, he submitted a list of those killed in the uprising. This list, dated September 11, 1680, and prepared in El Paso, was discovered in the Archives of the Indies and has become a definitive roll of those killed. Father Ayeta gives the place of origin of each missioner and the year of his arrival in New Mexico, with the one exception of Father Lorenzana. While he records this priest as coming from Galicia in Spain, he gives no date for his arrival in the new mission. Father de Talbán, a former *custos*, was from Seville, Spain, and had been in New Mexico since 1661. Father de Montesdoca was a Mexican native from Queretaro and had been in New Mexico since 1674.

The three missioners were attacked in their friary of Santo Domingo, a Queres pueblo on the Rio Grande, one of the oldest missions. The missioners tried to barricade themselves in their friary but were overcome and dragged into the adjoining church, where they were put to death. Their bodies were left there, piled in a heap. Two weeks later, Spanish refugees, retreating from Santa Fe, found the three corpses and buried them.

57. Father Juan de Jesús, Franciscan

Adjoining Santo Domingo was the pueblo of San Diego, inhabited by Jemez Indians, whom the Spanish called Xemes. The pastor was Father de Jesús, who came from Granada in Michóacan, Mexico. He had been in New Mexico since 1667. His mission included five smaller Jemez pueblos near Santo Domingo. There are no details on his death.

58. Father Lucas Maldonado, Franciscan

Father Maldonado is not included in the Ayeta list, which has twenty names although it states there were twenty-one martyrs, and his omission is taken to be an oversight. Father Maldonado is included in the list of Dr. Ysidro Sarinana, who delivered a funeral oration in Mexico City, on March 20, 1681. The name is also on other lists from the period, as well as in archival records.

Father Maldonado was pastor of the famous Acoma pueblo, located atop a high butte, now in the Gallup Diocese. He was killed there. It is possible he was killed on August 11, because of the distance of Acoma from the center of the revolt.

59. Father Juan del Val, Franciscan

This priest was from Val in Castile, Spain. He arrived in New Mexico in 1671. At the time of his death he was pastor of Purisima Concepción Mission at Alona (Halona), a Zuni pueblo near the Arizona border. Like Father Maldonado, he may have been killed August 11.

60. Father José de Espeleta, Franciscan
61. Father Augustín de Santa María, Franciscan

Father de Espeleta was a veteran of three decades of mission work. A native of Estella, Navarre, Spain, he was pastor of the Moqui (Hopi) mission of San Miguel at Oraibi. He was assisted by Father de Santa María from Pascuaro, Mexico, who had arrived in the mission in 1674. The American bishops' report gives the probable date of their death as August 11, again allowing for the distance a runner would have to come.

62. Father José de Figueroa, Franciscan

Father Figueroa was born in Mexico City and arrived in the northern mission in 1674. He was pastor of San Bernardo Mission in Aguatubi (Awatobi), a Moqui village, where he was killed, probably on August 11.

63. Father José de Trujillo, Franciscan

Death came to Father de Trujillo, from Cádiz, Spain, at the friary of St. Bartholomew, in the Moqui village of

Shongopovi (Xongopavi). He had worked in the Philippines before going to New Mexico in 1674. Before he left Manila, the abbess of the Poor Clare convent there told him that he would win a martyr's crown in his new assignment. Shortly after his arrival among the Moquis, he wrote a confrere in Mexico that the Blessed Virgin, who had healed a crippled Indian girl, told the child that with a few years the land would be destroyed because it had little respect for priests. For Father Trujillo, this prediction came true with his death on August 11.

Sources:
CCCMUS
Habig, Marion, *Heroes of the Cross*

Most modern writings on the Great Pueblo Revolt of 1680 depend on the transcripts made by historian Herbert E. Bolton of 486 pages of reports he located in the Mexican archives. Also prime source material are Ayeta's report and Vetancurt's *Menologia* (1698) and his *History of the Holy Gospel Province of Mexico* (1697).

Illinois

64. Father Gabriel de la Ribourde, Franciscan (1680)
Protomartyr of Illinois

Father Gabriel de la Ribourde was already well along in years when he came to the New World as a missioner. Born in France in 1615, he was the last in the male line of a noble and wealthy family in Burgundy. Renouncing his heritage, he joined the Recollect Franciscans, where he was known for his virtue, good humor, prudence, and generosity. He served his order in various capacities, notably as novice master and superior. When the Recollects were allowed to return to Canada in 1670, having been expelled by the British in 1629, he volunteered to go there despite his age. Because of his experience, he was appointed first commissary provincial and superior of the new mission.

Father de la Ribourde first labored in the Canadian capital of Quebec City, where he also served as confessor to Governor Frontenac. When his term as superior ended, he went as a missioner to Fort Frontenac (Kingston, Ontario), where Robert Cavalier de la Salle was commander. The explorer and the priest soon became close friends. De la Salle had the grand ambition to explore the western frontier, to follow the Mississippi to its end, and to claim the country for France. The expedition was authorized in 1679, and Father de la Ribourde offered to go along as senior chaplain. Two other Franciscans were chosen to assist him — Father Zenobe Membré and a former novice the old man had trained, Father Louis Hennepin, discoverer of Niagara Falls.

The expedition crossed Lake Ontario to Niagara Falls, and above this barrier the soldiers built a new vessel, *Griffin*, which they sailed across Lake Erie, up the Detroit River, across Lake Clair, into Lake Huron, down Lake Michigan, past the site of today's Chicago, and then built a fort on the Michigan side of the lake. The explorers ascended the St. Joseph River to the present South Bend, portaged to the Kankakee River and followed this and the Illinois River to a camp of Peoria Indians, near the present City of Peoria. It was no easy journey for the hardy soldiers, and it was particularly difficult for the aging priest, who never complained but remained always cheerful and encouraging.

Below the Peoria village, La Salle built Fort Crevecoeur, the first white settlement in Illinois. Father de la Ribourde went to this fort as its chaplain. Father Membré remained among the Peorias to do missionary work. Father Hennepin was dispatched by La Salle in the early spring of 1680 to explore the upper Mississippi. The commandant himself led a party back to Fort Frontenac for supplies. While he was gone, the soldiers left behind at Fort Crevecoeur deserted and fled, carrying away what was of value. Father de la Ribourde, who was unable to prevent the mutiny, returned to Father Membré to assist him in the work of conversion among the Illinois Indians, which was difficult because the Indians did not want to give up immoral practices. In September, Iroquois Indians from the east appeared in the area, raiding Illinois villages. Father Membré tried to arrange a peace without success. The Iroquois ordered the white men to leave the Peoria village, and the six Frenchmen, knowing they could offer no resistance, decided that it was prudent to go back to one of the French forts on the Great Lakes, where they could wait for La Salle's return.

September 18, 1680, saw the six white men paddling their canoe up the Illinois River. The party consisted of Father de la Ribourde; Father Membré; Henri Tonti, son of a banker and chief aid to La Salle; a Parisian youth, Etienne Renault, and two other Frenchmen who had been left by La Salle as guards. They had few supplies, little ammunition, and a rickety canoe. They camped the first night on the bank, and on the 19th they resumed their journey. Around noon, about twenty miles from the Peoria village, their canoe sprang a leak. They put into shore to repair the craft. Father de la Ribourde climbed the bank to stroll in some meadows and groves and say his breviary. He never returned, and in late afternoon when Tonti went seeking him, the Frenchmen found many Indian footprints and could only conclude that the priest had been captured. The travelers waited until the next day, building a great blaze during the night and firing scarce ammunition. When they realized the elderly priest was not coming back, they resumed their journey. It took them until December 4 to reach the safety of a fort at Green Bay, Wisconsin. It was not until much later that reports from various sources revealed what happened to the old man.

Father de la Ribourde had walked into a grove saying his office, unaware of any danger. Unknown to him, a Kickapoo war party had come from southern Wisconsin to attack the invading Iroquois. A scouting party of three young braves had been sent ahead, and these Indians spotted the French priest. They waited until he was abreast of them and then sprang from ambush, killing him instantly with war clubs. They scalped him, left the body, taking only his breviary, and returned to the main body of Kickapoos, where they held a victory war dance with the scalp. These facts were determined by a Jesuit missioner among the Kickapoos who found Father La Ribourde's breviary in a Kickapoo village and learned how it arrived there. In 1682 Father Hennepin was told by some Illinois Indians that they had come upon Father La Ribourde's body and recognized him as the kindly Greycoat who had worked among them. They buried his remains in the Illinois manner, somewhere in the vicinity of Seneca, a small Illinois town.

Sources:
CCCMUS
Habig, Marion, *Heroes of the Cross*

Texas

65. Father Zenobe Membré, Franciscan (1689)
66. Father Maxim le Clercq, Franciscan
67. Father Chefdeville, Sulpician

Through its exploration and occupation, Spain claimed possession of the southern and southwestern part of what is now the United States. However, France infringed on this ownership when Robert Cavalier Sieur de la Salle explored the Mississippi and claimed the entire valley for France in 1682. Two years later, he led a new expedition with the purpose of founding a French colony in this region. After an adventuresome voyage, the French explorer reached Matagorda Bay, Texas, on February 14, 1685. La Salle built Fort St. Louis on the bank of a creek that fed into the upper part of Matagorda Bay. Three priests were to remain at the fort along with the settlers while La Salle and his party went searching for the Mississippi, during which time a mutiny cost him his life. The priests who were left behind to care for the settlers and work among the Indians were two Franciscans, Father Zenobe Membré, who had been La Salle's chaplain in 1682, and Father Maxim le Clercq; and a Sulpician, the Abbé Chefdeville. Fort St. Louis continued to exist under great difficulties after La Salle's death. The Karankawa Indians of the region frequented the fort, and when a group of them entered the fort in mid-January 1689, no one thought anything of it. While these Indians distracted the French, a large body of Karankawas emerged from hiding and fell upon the unsuspecting French, massacring all but five who were taken captive as slaves. Among the dead were the three priests. This ended French penetration of Texas, and as a result Spaniards began to settle and Christianize the area.

Sources:
CCCMUS
Habig, Marion, *Heroes of the Cross*
Shea, John G., *The Catholic Church in Colonial Days*
Habig, Marion, *The Franciscan Père Marquette*

68. Stephen Tegananokoa, Iroquois (1690)
69. Frances Gonannhatenha, Iroquois (1692)
70. Margaret Garangouas, Iroquois (1692)

Many Christian Canadian Indians, not only of the Huron and Algonquin tribes but even converts from the Iroquois confederation, were put to death by the Iroquois out of hatred for Christianity. According to information furnished by a Jesuit missioner, himself a captive who later returned to Montreal, three from New York State stand out and are included in the document made by the American bishops for the Holy See.

In 1690, Stephen Tegananokoa was captured by a Cayuga war party, was taken to Onondaga, and was put to torture there, near Auriesville, where Isaac Jogues had died. A fervent Christian from the Sault St. Louis Mission, he was reproached by his Iroquois captors for deserting his village and becoming a "mission Christian." He replied, "I am a Christian and I am proud to be one. Do with me what you will." Some Indians began to beat him, shouting, "Pray." When he made the Sign of the Cross, his captors hacked off his fingers. When he began again, they severed his hand, all the while raining blows. Knowing the end was near, he commended his soul to God and then received a death blow.

Two years later an Onondoga woman, Frances Gonannhatenha, was put to terrible torture for becoming a Christian. She had been baptized at Onondaga but, knowing she could not practice her new faith there, went with her husband to Sault St. Louis. Some relatives, Indian braves, went after her. She was captured near the Sault, returned to Onondaga, and was given to the care of her sister, but when she refused to give up her religion, the sister had her put to torture. A kinsman tore the cross from her that she wore around her neck and cut a deep cross into her flesh. "Thank you, brother," she replied. "The cross you tore from me I might lose, but you have given me one I can keep, even in death." When she urged her tribesmen to become Christians, they fell upon her. They seared her body with red-hot gun barrels, scalped her, and covered her bleeding head with burning coals. She had endured the torture for three days when it was finally ended by her being stoned to death.

Likewise, the Onondagas did not spare Margaret Garangouas, even though she was the daughter of Tododaho, the hereditary chief. Margaret, too, was captured and taken prisoner to her village, where she was beaten and slashed with knives and then given time to recant her new faith. When three days had passed and she still refused, she was again put to torture, with only the names "Jesus, Mary, Joseph" escaping her lips. The torture lasted from noon to sunset, and when she was still firm in her faith, she was scalped and burned to death. The year was probably 1692.

Sources:
CCCMUS
Shea, John G., *The Church in Colonial Days*

Martyrs of the Second Pueblo Revolt, June 4, 1696

New Mexico

71. Father Francisco de Jesús María Casañas, Franciscan
72. Father José de Arbizu, Franciscan
73. Father Antonio de Carbonel, Franciscan
74. Father Francisco Corvera, Franciscan
75. Father Antonio Moreno, Franciscan

Following the Great Pueblo Revolt of 1680, the missions of New Mexico and Arizona lay desolate for some years. However, when Diego de Vargas completed the reconquest in 1692, seventeen Franciscans went northward from Mexico to reestablish the main mission centers and win back the converts that their martyred brethren had made years earlier. They were successful in their efforts, and once more the priests earned the jealousy and enmity of the pueblo medicine men. Once again these shamans plotted the ouster of the missioners. On June 4, 1696, the Second Pueblo Revolt took place, and this one cost the lives of five Franciscans.

Father Francisco de Jesús María Casañas was stationed in the pueblo of San Diego de los Xemes, among the Jemez Indians. It was the same mission where Father Juan de Jesús had died. Father Casañas was born in Barcelona, Spain, in 1656, and when he was fourteen he entered the Franciscan Order. After his ordination in 1682, he was recruited for the missionary college at Queretaro, Mexico. He was assigned to preaching, was stationed for a period in Merida, Yucatan, and worked as a missioner in Campeche. In 1690 he was chosen to go to Texas and help in the establishment of missions there among the Tejas Indians. Two years later he returned to Mexico to get supplies and complain about the bad example set by Spanish soldiers. However, he was one of eight missioners assigned to accompany de Vargas on the reconquest of New Mexico. The reconquest was without incident, and Father Casañas was placed in charge of Jemez pueblo, where he rebuilt the church and rectory and began winning back apostate Indians.

Despite rumblings of unrest, he continued on in his work. On the morning of June 4, 1696, he was called from his rectory to attend a dying man. The call was a ruse, and when he was outside the pueblo he was surrounded by Indians. One of them split his skull with a tomahawk blow, and the Indians then pelted his body with stones until he was covered by them. After the murder the Indians set fire to the church and rectory.

At the Tanos pueblo of San Cristóbal, near Galisteo, Fathers José de Arbizú and Antonio de Carbonel were killed. Father Francisco Corvera, pastor of the Tewa pueblo of San Ildefonso, was being visited by a neighbor, Father Antonio Moreno from Nambe Mission, when the mission was attacked by Tewas. They sealed the windows and door of the friary and set it afire. The two priests perished in the smoke and flames. The Indians also burned the church.

The 1696 revolt was more limited than the earlier one in 1680, and only three missions were affected. It was the end of insurrections. In succeeding years, the destroyed missions were reestablished and extended. The one tribe that resisted conversion, even to this day, has been the Hopis.

Sources:
CCCMUS
Habig, Marion, *Heroes of the Cross*
Unpublished notes
Hewett and Fisher, *Mission Monuments of New Mexico*

Florida

76. Father Luís Sánchez, Franciscan (1696)

Early in 1696 a group of twenty Franciscans arrived in St. Augustine, Florida, to staff new missions among the Jororo Indians. Settlements were made at Jororo, Mayaca, San José, San Antonio and Anacapi. Father Luís Sánchez was put in charge of the mission at Mayaca, south of St. Augustine. In October of that year, Indians rose up and destroyed a number of these missions. Father Sánchez was killed along with one Spanish soldier and five Indian converts.

The surviving missioners had to withdraw to St. Augustine. Later a new attempt was made, and a report from the Franciscan provincial, dated August 15, 1698, stated that the new missions were thriving. Ruins of the Misión de Jororo still can be found near New Smyrna, Florida, where a bronze plaque has been erected.

Sources:
CCCMUS
Habig, Marion, *Heroes of the Cross*
Kenny, Michael, *The Romance of the Floridas*

Virginia

77. Father Christopher Plunkett, Capuchin (1697)

Alexander Plunkett, born into a prominent Irish family at Donsaghly in 1649, entered the Capuchin Order at Charleville, France, in 1670, receiving the name Christopher. In the year 1680 he went to Virginia, possibly to center his missionary work at the estate of a kinsman, John Plunkett. It was dangerous work because the Protestants who governed Virginia were extremely anti-Catholic, and before long a price was put on his head. He was eventually captured, and after the English failed to make a Calvinist preacher out of him, they imprisoned him. He died from the harsh treatment of his captivity.

The *Annals* of the Irish Capuchins, written in 1741 and preserved in the Capuchin archives in Rome, has this to say about his labors: "Penetrating deeply into the remote villages and inhospitable forests, he approached timid Catholics who had been frightened by the pressure of persecution. He encouraged them by his eloquent words and instilled in them resignation and faith in the power and goodness of God. And to many who had been ensnared by that erroneous doctrine he brought light and explanation, so that he not only strengthened the holy faith of the many Catholics who had fallen into this deception, but even converted heretics and brought them into the bosom of the Catholic Church.

"And although he was careful to avoid the snares of the Protestant princes who brutally ruled the whole island, he fell into their hands and was harshly treated. Relentlessly they dragged him from one to another galley, with beatings and with sufferings from hunger and thirst. . . .

"Seeing, therefore, that they were not able to defeat and subdue him, they condemned him to exile, confining him to a barbarous island on which there was no one but heretics and enemies of Catholics. In that place the invincible Father Christopher saw sorrow, until he ended the captivity of men by passing into the sweet and perpetual liberty of God. He died alone and abandoned on that brutal island in the forty-eighth year of his age and the twenty-seventh in religion. His death is registered in the year 1697."

It is the opinion of historians that his death was caused by the treatment given him by the English. He may have died on an island in Chesapeake Bay, although the Irish references to Virginia as an island and to "barbarous island" cannot be assumed, since documents of the time also refer to Maryland as an island. Geography at that period was somewhat uncertain.

Sources:
CCCMUS
Habig, Marion, *Heroes of the Cross*

Mississippi

78. Father Nicholas Foucault (1701)
Protomartyr of Mississippi

The Parish Foreign Mission Society opened a seminary in Quebec, Canada, to train priests for the Western Indian missions. This caused some friction with the Jesuits, who looked upon the field as their own, just as some friction existed years earlier with the Franciscan Recollets for the same reason. The Canadian seminary chose the Mississippi Valley as its prime field.

Among the missioners sent there was Father Nicholas Foucault. It is not clear whether he was a Paris Foreign Missioner or a member of the diocesan clergy. He was a pastor in Quebec when he volunteered to go among the Arkansas Indians, where other Quebec missioners were at work under the sponsorship of the Foreign Mission Seminary. He worked two years there among the Arkansas, suffering much from their inhospitality. In July 1702, he left to visit the French settlement at Mobile. In the vicinity of Fort Adams, Mississippi, he was slain by his Indian guides. Father Antoine Davion, a missioner in the Fort Adams area who investigated the incident, reported the death to Bishop Vallier in Quebec, saying that the murder was probably instigated by the Arkansas' hatred of the priest and his Christian teachings.

Source: CCCMUS

The Florida Martyrs of 1704

The settlement of Jamestown brought the English to the New World with their hatred of the Spanish and things Catholic. From Jamestown they moved south, and when a settlement was made at Charleston, South Carolina, the death watch of the Guale missions began. Although the Spanish had rights by discovery and occupancy, their Florida settlements became the prey of Carolinian troops, their Indian allies, and English pirates who plundered coastal settlements. From 1680 on, these attacks were stepped up, with the Spanish unable to offer real resistance. Christian Indians fled into the forests. The Golden Islands were exploited in raid after raid. The Spanish governor withdrew Indians and missioners from St. Catherine's to Sapelo, then to Amelia Island, and then to San Juan on St. John's River.

Avid for slaves and plunder, and with a burning hatred for the "papist religion," South Carolina's Governor Moore organized an army of pagan Indians under English officers and sent them southward while he himself led a fleet against St. Augustine. The missions were pillaged and burned. Churches, schools, and *conventos* went up in flames after being looted for valuables. The valuable Franciscan library, the most important collection of recorded knowledge in eastern America, was burned and "the Holy Bible did not escape because it was in Latin." Some 1,400 Apalache Indians were captured and taken north to be sold in the slave markets of Charleston. Those Christian missioners who did not escape the English were treated with brutal contempt.

Florida

79. Father Juan Parga Arraiyo, Franciscan
80. Antonio Enixa, Indian Layman
81. Amador Cuipa Feliciano, Indian Layman
82. Father Domingo Criado, Franciscan
83. Father Tiburcio de Osorio, Franciscan
84. Father Augustín Ponce de León, Franciscan

Father Juan Parga and two Indian companions were tortured and slain on January 25, 1704, near Tallahassee, Florida, at the Misión La Concepción de Ayubale. He was burned at the stake, beheaded, and had one of his legs hacked off. The historian, John Gilmary Shea writes, "The martyrdom of Ayubale has no parallel in our annals except the deaths of Father Brébeuf, Lalemant, Daniel and Garnier, in Huron country [Canada], which has been so often pathetically described; but the butcheries perpetrated there were before the eyes and at the order of the Governor of a

Christian colony." The Catholic Indians were treated in like manner. Following the raid, Father Juan de Villaba returned to the devastated area and found houses demolished and cultivated fields destroyed; bodies of men and women were scalped, mutilated, and burned, many still hanging from stakes. He recovered Father Parga's mangled remains and brought them to Ybithachucu for burial. Survivors told of the bravery of the Indians Antonio Enixa and Amador Cuipa Feliciano, both of the Misión San Luís, who showed a heroism reminiscent of early Christian martyrs.

While the exact date of the other martyrdoms is not certain, all died at approximately the same time as Father Parga. Father Manuel de Mendoza was shot through the head. Father de Villaba had his body half consumed by fire, his beads and partly melted crucifix having burned into his flesh. Father Blas Placido, the superior of the Franciscan friary of St. Augustine, listed the other dead as Father Domingo Criado, a Spaniard; Father Tiburcio de Osorio, a Cuban; and Father Agustín Ponce de León, who was born in Florida and thus became the first American-born priest to become a martyr.

The bishops' list that was submitted to Rome included the name of Brother Mark Delgado, based, probably, on his inclusion in *The Romance of the Floridas*, along with Father Angel Miranda. Neither name is on the list of Father Placido, and Father Miranda is mentioned in another account as being at Nombre de Dios Mission, near St. Augustine, in 1712, and he later became a Franciscan provincial councillor. While Brother Delgado was with Father Parga, the best opinion is that he escaped death.

Many of the Christian Indians who survived the Moore raid moved to Mobile for safety. While the Spanish settlements in Florida continued for some years, the Indian missions never recovered from the devastation Governor Moore had wrought.

Sources:
CCCMUS
Kenny, Michael, *The Romance of the Floridas*
Habig, Marion, *Heroes of the Cross*

Louisiana

85. Father Jean François Buisson de Saint Cosmé (1706)
Protomartyr of Louisiana

In September 1698, Father Jacques Gravier, S.J., wrote from San Ignace Mission at Michilimackinac that three priests of the Quebec Foreign Mission Seminary had arrived there on the way to the lower Mississippi missions to the south. They were the pioneer band from the Quebec seminary. They were Father Antoine Davion, who was to report the martyrdom of Father Foucault; Father François Jolliet de Montigny, a Frenchman, ordained in Quebec in 1693, chaplain of the Ursuline convent there, and soon, after his American mission tour, to go to China; and Father Jean François Buisson de Saint Cosmé, who was born in Quebec in 1667. He was ordained at twenty-three years of age and worked as a missioner in Acadia before being assigned to the Mississippi region.

Father Gravier's letter indicates that the Quebec priests were unfamiliar with the Indian language. At another Illinois Jesuit mission they spent the winter, leaving in the spring with a gift of seven sacks of corn. Thus prepared, the newcomers went on to their new posts. Father Buisson worked first at Cahokia and then in the Natchez area. Late in the year 1706, he was traveling down river when he was murdered by a band of Chetimacha Indians in the territory that is now Louisiana, as he was approaching the mouth of the Mississippi.

Sources:
CCCMUS
Habig, Marion, unpublished notes
Jesuit Relations, Vol. 65; pp. 59, 83, 262

Michigan

86. Father Constantine Delhalle, Franciscan (1706)

Although Father Constantine Delhalle died in the course of his duties, trying to make peace between two Indian tribes, he was not killed in *odium fidei*. However, since he is on the official American list and he died by violence, he is included here.

Father Delhalle, a saintly man of exemplary life, was a professor of philosophy in Flanders when he went to Canada as a missioner in 1701. That same summer La Motte Cadillac was appointed commandant of Detroit and the areas to the west of it. Cadillac organized soldiers and settlers to go with him to Detroit and included two priests, Father Vallant du Gueslis, a Jesuit, to work among the Indians, and Father Delhalle to care for the troops and the French settlers. On July 21, 1701, Detroit was founded, and within a week Father Delhalle began building a church, which he named in honor of St. Anne.

In 1706, a conflict began between the Miamis and Ottawas, and Detroit sided with the Miamis. An Ottawa chief asked Father Delhalle to go to the fort and ask the soldiers to cease firing at them, since the Ottawas had no quarrel with the French. Father Delhalle agreed, and as he approached the fort he was joined by some Miamis. The Ottawas opened fire on their enemies, and a bullet struck the priest, killing him instantly. Father Delhalle was buried in his church, which was later razed in another war, and in 1723 was reinterred in a new church within the fort.

Sources:
CCCMUS
Habig, Marion, *Heroes of the Cross*

Alabama

87. Father Jacques Gravier, Jesuit (1708)
Protomartyr of Alabama

Father Jacques Gravier, S.J., was an outstanding missioner of the western tribes. For a time he was superior of the St. Ignace Mission at Michillimackinac and vicar general of the western regions for the Bishop of Quebec. He composed an Illinois dictionary and traveled the area from St. Ignace to the mouth of the Mississippi. His letters in the *Jesuit Relations* only give a hint of the trials he endured.

Father Gravier was born in Moulins, France, in 1651. He was educated by the Jesuits and entered the Society in Paris in 1670. After ordination, he passed some time teaching until in 1685 he went to Canada. He spent the first year at Sillery and then went to the western missions, where he became known for his linguistic abilities and his missionary talents. A great deal of his time in the western missions was spent alone and apart from his brother Jesuits.

In 1705 Father Gravier was working among the Peoria Indians, where he was opposed by medicine men and warriors who preferred vice to virtue and superstition to sanctity. Some of these enemies waylaid him, and he was wounded from arrows in five places. In one wound the arrow was embedded, causing blood poisoning. When the wound did not heal, he made an agonizing journey downriver to Mobile, where there was an army surgeon. The doctor could do nothing for him and recommended that he return to France for help. He did get treatment in Paris, but the wound would not heal. Despite this, he wrote the Jesuit

Superior General that although the wound inflicted for teaching the Catholic faith was hastening his end, he was returning to his poor Illinois because he had promised God to die among them.

The wounded missioner arrived back at Mobile on February 12, 1708, and was asked by Governor Bienville to remain there until after Easter so that the garrison might have Easter services and make their paschal duties. He died there on Dauphin Island (L'Isle Massacre) in Mobile Bay, not far from the present city of Mobile, Alabama, on April 23, 1708, as a result of the wound. There is much contemporary evidence that he received the wound in hatred of the faith and that he died as a result of it.

Sources:
CCCMUS
Jesuit Relations, vol. 65, pp. 53, 101, 264; vol. 66, pp/ 50, 124, 245, 256

Wisconsin

88. Father Léonard Vatier, Franciscan (1715)
Protomartyr of Wisconsin

Details are lacking on Father Vatier, who was a missioner working out of Detroit. He was captured by Indians in that area in 1707, and it is reported that he was killed by Fox Indians in Wisconsin in 1715.

Sources:
CCCMUS
Cigognani, A.G., *Sanctity in America*

89. Father Juan Mínguez, Franciscan (1720)
Protomartyr of Nebraska

Learning that French troops had advanced to the area of the Platte River, known to the Spaniards as the Rio de Jesus María, Governor Valverde of New Mexico ordered that a presidio be established there and that a Spanish colony should be begun in Kansas. He organized an expedition to accomplish these ends and appointed Pedro de Villasur to head it. Villasur left New Mexico with forty soldiers, seventy Indians, some settlers and traders, and two chaplains, Father Juan de Dios and Father Juan Mìnguez. The latter was a veteran missioner, having served in Santa Fe, Zuni, Nambe and Santa Clara.

The party reached the Platte early in August. On August 12, as they were breaking camp, they were suddenly attacked from ambush by Pawnees. The battle was over quickly, and when it was done forty-five lay dead, among them Villasur and Father Mínguez. A few escaped to make known the massacre, including Father Juan de Dios, who was later captured and then ransomed. From the descriptions that have come down to us, it does not seem that Father Mínguez was a martyr but a victim of war; however, since he is on the bishops' list, he is included here.

Sources:
CCCMUS
Habig, Marion, *Heroes of the Cross*

90. Brother José Pita, Franciscan (1721)

Again the list of the American bishops has a name that is doubtful in a list of martyrs. He is Brother José Pita, who was killed by Apaches in 1721 in east Texas along with a companion. The two Spaniards were hunting buffalo when the Apaches found them. It is true the Apaches were enemies of the Spanish and their religion, but there is no evidence that Brother José's death was in *odium fidei*. Later his remains were recovered and brought to San Antonio for burial. The place of his death was near Rockdale.

Sources:
CCCMUS
Habig, Marion, *Heroes of the Cross*
    Unpublished notes

Maine

91. Father Sebastien Rale, Jesuit (1724)
Protomartyr of Maine

The first missioner to die violently in Maine was Brother Gilbert du Thet, S.J., who was stationed on Mount Desert Island and worked among the Abenaki Indians with Father Claude Quentin and Father Charles Lalemant. In 1613, only a year after he had arrived in Canada, he was killed when English from Virginia under Argall attacked the mission, which had been founded only months before. The two priests were taken as prisoners to Virginia and later repatriated to France. Brother du Thet was buried on the island, the first Catholic mission in New England. Since the attack was primarily against the French post established on the island and the captured priests were released, Brother Gilbert's death does not seem to be in hatred of the Faith, although the English had no love for Catholics. Therefore, the role of protomartyr of Maine properly belongs to Father Sebastien Rale, S.J., who was killed a century later.

There are some difficulties with a biographical sketch of Father Rale, whose name is also found as Rasle, Rasles and Racles. The notes in the *Jesuit Relations* give the Rale spelling, and this is generally followed. He was born at Pontarlier, Besançon, France, either on January 4, 1657, or January 20, 1654. Based on other dates within the Society of Jesus, the first date seems the more probable. He entered the Jesuit novitiate at Dole, Lyons, in 1675. He finished his studies in 1688 and sailed the following year for New France with a party under Frontenac. His first assignment was to an Abenaki village near Quebec. In 1691 he was assigned to the Illinois Indians in the west, but he was recalled after two years and in 1694 went to work among the Abenakis along the Kennebec River in Maine. He was to remain there for the rest of his life, becoming an authority on this Indian tribe, composing an Abenaki dictionary, the manuscript of which was seized by his English murderers and is preserved today at Harvard University. He also translated prayers and hymns into Abenaki, and a catechism he wrote was used for many years.

Father Rale's mission, the Assumption of Our Lady, was founded in 1646 by another Jesuit, Father Gabriel Druillettes. The Abenakis proved receptive to the Faith, and the solid roots these missioners put down remain until today. In a letter to his nephew in France a few years before his death, Father Rale wrote how he had built a church "commodious and well adorned" that was as well equipped as churches in Europe. He spoke of his native choir of forty young Indians "who in cassocks and surplices assist at divine Service; each one has his duty, not only in serving at the holy Sacrifice of the Mass, but in chanting the divine Office at the Benediction of the blessed Sacrament and in the Processions." The Indians loved processions and arrived from miles around to take part in them. The Indians came to church twice a day — each morning for Mass and again at sunset for night prayers.

Father Rale was much loved by his charges. He took care of himself and his house entirely on his own, using no Indian as a servant. He continually fasted, ate no meat or fish, drank no wine, and subsisted mainly on a corn soup that he made himself. He spent his days catechizing the young people, attending the sick, receiving the Indians who "come to me with their griefs and anxieties," attending council meetings at which the chiefs sought his advice. The result, Father Rale wrote, was that the whole Abenaki nation was Catholic "and very zealous in preserving its Religion." This Catholicity was anathema to the neighboring English Puritans.

The English made many overtures to the Abenakis but were continually turned down. Then they began raiding this peaceful people. They looked upon Father Rale as an obstacle to their plan "of gradually seizing this land which is between [New] England and Acadia." "They have attempted to remove me from my flock," he wrote, "and more than once a price has been set on my head." In 1722 the English raided the mission. Abenaki scouts saw them coming and warned the priest. He consumed the Hosts and hid the sacred vessels. He wrote, "They were within gunshot when we descried them; all I could do was plunge with haste into the forest. But as I had no time to take my snowshoes, and as, besides, I still experienced great weakness caused by a fall — in which, some years ago, my thigh and leg were broken — it was not possible for me to run very far." However, the English did not find him hiding in the woods. When he returned to his village, he found his house and church pillaged.

Father Rale had no thought of escaping to the safety of

Canada. "What will become of the flock, if it be deprived of its Shepherd? Death alone can separate me from them," he wrote, adding, "I do not consider my life more precious than myself." In another letter, written to his brother the year before his murder, he stated, "I have the most to fear from the English Gentlemen of our neighborhood. It is true that they long ago resolved on my death; but neither their ill will toward me, nor the death with which they threaten me, can ever separate me from my old flock." He was well into his sixties when he wrote that, but he had the determination of a young priest. The New England governor tried to separate the Indians from the priest, promising them great benefits if they would accept reform ministers instead of Father Rale. The chiefs sent back the reply, "No, we hold to the Prayer [Catholic Faith] forever."

The Puritans decided to wait no longer. They assembled a force of English settlers, some soldiers, and Mohawk allies, and struck without warning on August 23, 1724. The men of Norridgewock were away on a hunt; only women, children, and old men were left, and they could offer no defense. Father Rale, calling on the people to flee to the woods, ran quickly in front of the church to draw the enemy's attention. Beneath a large cross he had raised, the old man was cut down in a hail of bullets. Not satisfied, the enemy scalped him, smashed in his skull, and mutilated his body by hacking it with knives. They then burned his church and rectory, carrying off his scalp and sacred vessels, along with the private papers he had. The box containing the papers is now in the possession of the Maine Historical Society, and the dictionary is at Harvard. (A footnote in the *Jesuit Relations* sets the date of martyrdom as August 19. However, the bishops' list and others place it on August 23.)

Sources:
CCCMUS
Jesuit Relations, Vol. 67, pp 85ff, 133ff, 338

Shea, John G., *History of the Catholic Church in the United States I*, pp. 538-602
The Church World (Portland, Maine), August 22, 1974

Texas

92. Brother Luís Montés de Oca, Franciscan (1726)

Brother Luís served as a procurator for the Franciscan Texas missions, bringing them supplies as needed. He was on his way to Misión Nuestra Senora del Espiritu Santo in 1726 when he perished in a prairie fire started by hostile Indians. The news of his death was received in Zacatecas, Mexico, in January of 1727. Some years later a memorial sent to the comissionary general in Spain by Francisco Vellejo, Guardian of the Zacatecas college, simply stated he "died in the flames of a fire started by Indians hostile to us." The dates given in the bishops' report are inaccurate on the basis of the above information. The place of death was in eastern Texas.

Sources:
CCCMUS
Habig, Marion, unpublished notes

Mississippi

93. Father Paul du Poisson, Jesuit (1729)

Father du Poisson was born in Epinal, France, January 27, 1692. He entered the Jesuits when he was twenty and after ordination volunteered for the Indian missions in 1726. He was assigned to work with the Arkansas Indians, whose language he learned in an unusually short time. His missionary efforts were very successful among the Arkansas, and in a letter he wrote: "I have consecrated all my strength and power to their conversion." In late November of 1729, after burying a Jesuit Brother who had died very suddenly, he went to Natchez, a French garrison post on the Mississippi, to attend to some business. Unknown to him, the Indians there were upset with the French. A letter from a Father Petit in New Orleans to the Jesuit procurator tells what happened. Father Petit writes:

"He arrived among the Natchez on the 26th of November, that is, two days before the massacre. The next day, which was the first Sunday of Advent, he said Mass in the parish and preached in the absence of the Curé. He was to return in the afternoon to his Mission among the Arkansas, but he was detained by some sick persons, to whom it was necessary to administer the Sacraments. On Monday, he was about to say Mass, and to carry the holy Viaticum to one of those sick persons whom he had confessed the evening before, when the massacre began; a gigantic chief, six feet in height, seized him and, having thrown him to the ground, cut off his head with blows of a hatchet. The Father in falling only uttered these words, 'Ah, my God! Ah, my God!' "

The Natchez Indians at the same time were killing those French who did not escape. They plundered the houses and warehouse. Some women were left alive as slaves, and two Frenchmen were spared.Those who escaped carried the news to New Orleans, but it was some months before the French regained control of Natchez. The dates given in the above letter are accepted by Shea and the bishops' report. Another writer states that the Jesuit archives give the date of Father du Poisson's death as December 31. If so, it would seem to be in error, since the Petit letter is quite precise, and it is doubtful if Father du Poisson would be away from his mission during the Christmas season.

Sources:
CCCMUS
Shea, John G., *History of the Catholic Missions*
Jesuit Relations, Vol. 67, pp. 277-325, 340; 68, p. 167

Mississippi

94. Father Jean Souel, Jesuit (1729)

Father Jean Souel, born in 1695, came from the same Jesuit province in France (Champagne) as did Father du Poisson. In fact, the two men arrived in the Indian missions of Louisiana together in 1726. While du Poisson went to work among the Natchez, Father Souel was assigned to the Yazoos in the present Vicksburg area. He also preached to the Corroy and Offogoula tribes. Because of his holiness, the Yazoos named him "Chief of Prayer." He won many converts but was also resented by some Indians because he condemned their sodomistic and other pagan practices, which the historian Charlevoix says "was probably the main cause of his death."

Some Yazoos, who had been at Natchez when Father du Poisson was murdered and who had been aroused by the Natchez against the French, were returning from that massacre on the evening of December 11, 1729, when they came upon Father Souel on the way to his mission house after visiting the Yazoo chief. Upon seeing the French priest, they opened fire on him, and Father Souel was killed in a ravine by musket balls.

Father Petit, in reporting the deaths of the two Jesuit missioners, noted that they were both disposed toward martyrdom and that this "has doubtless placed a great difference in God's eyes between their deaths and that of the others, who have fallen martyrs to the French name." He adds that both missioners were mourned by Indians who remained faithful to their Christian beliefs. (The report of the American bishops gives the date of the martyrdom as December 18, but we have followed the date given in the Petit letter and a footnote (Vol. 67, p. 341) in *Jesuit Relations*. This puts the death closer to Father du Poisson, and allows ample time for the Yazoos to have returned from Natchez.)

Sources:
CCCMUS
Jesuit Relations, Vol. 68, pp. 173, 185, 219; Vol. 69, p. 341
Shea, John G., *History of the Catholic Missions*

Illinois

95. Father Gaston (1730)

Cahokia, located near the present East St. Louis, Illinois, was the oldest French settlement in Illinois country. Founded in 1699, it was a French fur-trading center. In 1730, a newly ordained Father Gaston of the Quebec Foreign Mission Seminary arrived at Cahokia to do mission work among the nearby Tamarois (Tamara) Indians, an Illinois subtribe. He was killed by those Indians shortly after his arrival. Other details, including his full name, are not known. Cardinal Cicognani gives the date of his martyrdom as February 2, 1730, but this date is suspect, for it is doubtful that anyone would canoe and portage through the Great Lakes and then to the Mississippi in mid-winter.

Sources:
CCCMUS
Shea, John G., *The Catholic Church in Colonial Days*
Cicognani, Amleto, *Sanctity in America*

96. Father Domingo de Saraoz, Franciscan (1731)

Father de Saraoz was the pastor of the mission at Santa Ana pueblo, which numbered about 600 Indians. The mission was an important one because it served as a supply center for other New Mexico parishes. Father de Saraoz found his work handicapped by the licentiousness of many of the Indians, whom he severely criticized in his sermons. This won him the hatred of tribal medicine men, who conspired to poison his food, thus causing his death. The bishops' list has this happening in 1631, but according to unpublished notes of Father Marion Habig, the distinguished Franciscan historian, the event happened a century later, the exact date of death unknown.

Sources:
CCCMUS
Habig, Marion, unpublished notes

97. Father Antoine Senat, Jesuit
98. Commander Pierre d'Artiquette, French Layman
99. Captain François Marie Bissot de Vincennes, Canadian Layman
100. Captain Louis d'Ailebout de Coulonge, Canadian
101. Captain Louis Charles du Tisne, Canadian
102. Captain François Mariauchau d'Esgly, Canadian
103. Captain Pierre Antoine de Tonty, Canadian
104. Captain Louis Groston de St. Ange, Canadian
(All were put to death by the Chickasaws, March 25, 1736)

These names should probably not be included in this work, but they are listed here because they are on the official list of American martyrs submitted by the American bishops to the Holy See, and in that sense a decision has been made concerning them. The reason given by the bishops is that while they were put to death by the Chickasaw Indians, who captured them in battle, the Chickasaws were allied with the Protestant English and "appear to have hated not only the French but also the religion of the French." A similar argument could be made for Father Vincent Cappadano, a Maryknoll priest who was posthumously awarded the Medal of Honor for giving his life to minister during the Vietnam war, because the Communists who killed him hated religion; or for Father John Washington, another chaplain, who gave his life vest to another and chose to go down with his ship, torpedoed because Hitler hated both America and religion. Fathers Senat, Cappadono, and Washington were all in a sense martyrs to duty, but they died primarily because they were with soldiers in a battle zone and only remotely because they were Catholics. Even more so for the soldiers who died with those chaplains.

Father Senat entered the Jesuit Province of Toulouse in 1716. He was assigned to the Illinois missions in 1732 and began work there the following year. He gained fluency in the language, and this, accompanied by his own saintly character and zeal, won many converts. About this time the Chikasaws made a treaty with the English and began raiding French trading posts. The French organized soldiers to punish them and Father Senat went along as chaplain. Father Mathurin le Petit, Jesuit superior for Louisiana, reported to the Jesuit Superior General what happened: "For the purpose of giving spiritual assistance, he [Father Senat] accompanied an army composed of French and Indians against barbarians called Tchikakas, who are enemies of this colony. The result of this was unfortunate. Our men were either slain by the enemy or put to flight. Father Senat might, as many had done, have sought safety in flight; but refusing a horse that was offered him, he preferred yielding to the fury of the barbarians, rather than leave without spiritual succor the brave head of the army and the French, whom he saw stretched on the ground because of their wounds, or carried off by the enemy. . . . The barbarians, who rushed upon him in a body, as he was kneeling in prayer, were immediately seen showering blows from clubs upon their captive, the prelude to much greater torture."

Father Senat, the seven officers listed above, plus thirteen unnamed French soldiers, were beaten, tortured, and then condemned to die by fire. The priest confessed and absolved his French companions, leading them to the execution spot while reciting the *Miserere*. As the flames rose, Father Senat led the group in prayers and hymns, all dying bravely. The date of the executions was Palm Sunday, March 25, 1736. The settlement of Vincennes, Indiana, was named after one of the French officers who died with Father Senat.

Sources:
CCCMUS
Jesuit Relations, Vol. 68, pp 309-311, 328

105. Father Jean Pierre Aulneau, Jesuit (1736)
Protomartyr of Minnesota

Father Jean Piere Aulneau was born in the Vendée Department of France, April 21, 1705. Two of his brothers became priests and a sister a nun. He himself entered the Jesuits and in 1734 was sent to Canada to finish his fourth year of theology, be ordained there, and prepare for a missionary career. In a letter he wrote back to France, he told of the difficulties that awaited him. He would be stationed at Fort St. Charles, located in the northwest corner of Lake of the Woods, Minnesota, which the great explorer and trader Pierre Verendrye had established as France's westernmost outpost. Father Aulneau was to work among the Cree and Assinboine Indians, whose language he would have to learn and whose dictionary he would have to compile, for there was nothing written. He was also instructed to locate the Mandans, whom he called *ouantchipouanes* (the people who live in holes). He would be far removed from other priests. He asked his friend for prayers "to obtain for me all necessary grace to undergo hardships which Providence may hold in reserve for me for my sanctification." Perhaps with forevision, he wrote to another priest friend: "I should deem myself happy if I should be judged worthy of laying down my life for the One from whom I received it."

Father Aulneau left Montreal with Verendrye on June 21, 1735, reaching Fort St. Charles on September 6. It is not easy to sum up an incredible journey of almost three months of paddling and portage in a sentence, but, as one Jesuit noted, Father Aulneau had made "the longest, most painful and dangerous journey ever undertaken by a missioner in Canada." He spent the winter learning Indian languages, caring for the *voyageurs* and planning how to reach the tribes he had been directed to find. After a difficult winter, Verendrye decided to send a party back to Michillimackinac (now Mackinac Island) for supplies. Father Aulneau, who now knew his own needs better and was undoubtedly anxious to see a fellow priest for spiritual sustenance, went along. The group, under the command of Verendrye's twenty-year-old son, John Baptiste, left Fort Charles on June 5, 1736. They had only traveled twenty miles and had gone ashore on an island in the lake to make camp for the night when they were attacked by Sioux, searching for Cree enemies. What actually happened that day no one knows because no survivors were left.

Some days later, friendly Indians found the bodies and

covered them with stones. A trader arrived at Fort St. Charles from Montreal and reported that he had not passed the party en route. Verendrye, concerned, sent some men to follow the route his son would have taken, and the searchers came upon the remains on the island which from then on was called Massacre Island. The bodies of Jean Baptiste and Father Aulneau, along with the heads of the other *voyageurs* (all had been decapitated by the Sioux), were brought back to Fort Charles for burial. In the months that followed, various articles stolen from the slain men were recovered, among them a silver seal belonging to the murdered priest.

In 1758 the fur trade came to an end, and Fort St. Charles was abandoned as the English took over Canada. In time the location of the fort was forgotten, the graves of the dead were lost, and Father Aulneau passed into oblivion. In 1889 a Jesuit was giving a mission in the Vendée when he was approached by an old man who said his name was Aulneau and that he had some letters, 150 years old, that had been written by a Jesuit in his family. The visiting priest borrowed the letters, which were from Father Aulneau to various members of his family, plus letters from Jesuit friends telling how the young priest had died. The letters were eventually published in Canada and awakened interest both in Father Aulneau and Fort St. Charles. To make a long story short, after various expeditions and the weighing of Indian legends, both Massacre Island and Fort St. Charles were found, along with the bodies of Father Aulneau and Jean Baptiste Verendrye, each positively identified, the priest by his rosary and other items, Jean Baptiste by a wound. The remains, skeletons and skulls, were transferred to a Jesuit college in Manitoba, and a shrine was built at the site of the fort, which was recreated by the Knights of Columbus. A fire in 1921 at St. Boniface College, Manitoba, consumed the bones of Father Aulneau, so only a memory is left.

Sources:
CCCMUS
Shanahan, Emmett A., *Minnesota's Forgotten Martyr*
Jesuit Relations, Vol. 68, p. 237, 331

Texas

106. Father Francisco Xavier Silva, Franciscan (1749)

While on the way from San Antonio to Misión San Juan Bautista, and accompanied by soldiers, Father Silva and his party were attacked by Natages Apaches and all were killed. In a report sent to the Commissary General in Spain, Father Guardian Francisco Vallejo said that the missioner "was pierced by arrows and torn to pieces by the Apaches, whose ferocity was so great that they devoured his flesh." Father Habig reports that the slain priest had gone to get supplies for a new mission he was to open on the Nueces River, and that the Apaches sought to stop the work of the missioners and prevent new missions from opening. The bodies of the murdered Spaniards were found by friendly Indians, and Father Silva was buried at San Juan Bautista.

Sources:
CCCMUS
Habig, Marion, *Heroes of the Cross*
               Unpublished notes

Texas

107. Father José Francisco Ganzabal, Franciscan (1752)

Captain Felipe de Rabago, *comandante* of the presidio at San Xavier, was a dissolute man. When he took the wife of one of his soldiers, José Ceballos, for his own pleasure, he was excommunicated by the superior of the San Xavier missions, and Father Ganzabal nailed the excommunication on the presidio door. Rabago arrested Ceballos and, while holding him in prison, assaulted the man's wife before him. Ceballos finally escaped and took refuge in Misión Candelaria, but Rabago, ignoring the right of sanctuary, rode his horse into the mission chapel and seized the betrayed man. Ceballos was released ten days later, however, and returned to Candelaria when the missioners threatened to report this violation of sanctuary to Mexico City.

Finally, Rabago sent four soldiers to murder Ceballos and the priests. On the way they were joined by a renegade Indian, Andrés. The culprits arrived at the mission after dark. They saw Ceballos seated at a table with Fathers Ganazabal and Miguel Pinilla. Two shots rang out, and Ceballos fell to the floor, mortally wounded. While Father Pinilla bent over the dying man, Father Ganzabal snatched up the candle and rushed to the door. Andrés let go an arrow at the priest that pierced him under the left arm and entered his heart. Father Ganzabal dropped to the floor dead, and the candle went out, thus saving Father Pinilla.

Ceballos was killed because he stood in the way of Rabago. Father Ganzabal was slain because he had protested Rabago's debauchery and had posted the excommunication. Father Pinilla was to have been killed because he had issued the excommunication. Castenada, in his history of the Texas missions, says that there is no doubt that Father Ganzabal was martyred for his denunciation of the vices of Rabago and his soldiers. The date of the murder was May 11, 1752. Rabago was later taken as a prisoner to Mexico City, where, after some years and a number of trials, he was released for lack of evidence that he was personally involved.

Sources:
CCCMUS

Castenada, C.E., *Our Catholic Heritage in Texas* (translation of Juan Morfi's *Memorias*).

Habig, Marion, *Heroes of the Cross*

Texas

108. Father Alonso Giraldo de Terreros, Franciscan (1758)
109. Father José Santiesteban Aberin, Franciscan (1758)

These missioners were killed at San Saba Mission, near the present Menard, Texas, on March 16, 1758.

Father de Terreros was born in Cartagena, Huelva, Spain, on June 19, 1699, and entered the Franciscans at their college in Queretaro, Mexico, in 1721. After ordination, he was assigned to the Texas missions in 1728. Father Aberin was born in Navarre in 1719 and became a Franciscan in Pamplona. He was assigned to Mexico in 1749. These two priests, together with Father Miguel Molina, were stationed at San Saba Mission in 1758, a foundation that had been made to serve Christian Apaches and to work among those who were pagans.

Shortly after sunrise on March 16, a band of Comanche Indians, enemies of the Apaches, raided the mission. Father Aberin was preparing to say Mass when Father Molina warned him of what was happening. Father Terreros went to the mission gate to try to reason with the Comanches, but he was cut down by two bullets and also received a lance thrust. The invaders found Father Aberin, kneeling before the altar of the church, and they decapitated him there. Father Molina received a bullet wound in the chest, but he managed to escape with his life and recovered from his wound.

Sources:
CCCMUS
Habig, Marion, *Heroes of the Cross*
Unpublished notes

California

110. Father Luís Jayme, Franciscan (1775)
Protomartyr of California

When news of the martyrdom of Father Luís Jayme (the bishops' list misspells his name) at San Diego reached Father Junípero Serra at San Carlos Mission to the north, the founder of the California missions exclaimed, "Thanks be to God! That land is now watered. Now the conversation of the Diegueños will be accomplished!"

Father Luís Jayme was born on the island of Majorca, Spain, October 18, 1740, and was baptized Melchior. He entered the Franciscans in Palma in 1760, adopting the religious name of Luís. He taught philosophy for several years and in 1770 left Spain for America. In October of the same year he departed the Franciscan College in Mexico City with nine other friars and arrived at Monterey on May 21, 1771. There Father Serra assigned him to San Diego, the first mission the veteran Serra had founded in 1769. Father Jayme proposed to move the San Diego Mission from the vicinity of the presidio (the Old Town) to a nearby valley where it is presently situated. Father Serra approved the change, and Father Jayme began construction of the new building, effecting the transfer in August 1774.

Conversion work was slow but steady. The San Diego Indians were of Yuman stock and not as adaptable as other California tribes. The medicine men of the tribe exerted strong influence, realizing that their own position was jeopardized by the priests. Nevertheless, at the time of his

Father Luís Jayme, martyred in California, 1775

death Father Jayme counted 431 baptized Indians. Some of these Christians warned Father Jayme and his assistant, Father Vincente Fuster, that the medicine men were stirring up trouble, but the missioners were not alarmed since the shamans had always been hostile. Late on the night of November 5, 1775, hundreds of pagan Indians gathered around the mission. Father Jayme went out to meet them, giving the usual mission greeting: "Love God, my children."

Some Indians attacked him, dragging him off to a nearby arroyo, where he was clubbed to death and his body pierced with arrows. They also killed a Spanish blacksmith and a carpenter. They set fire to some mission buildings, ransacking their contents. By this time Spanish soldiers appeared and eventually drove off the raiders. Father Jayme's remains, hardly recognizable, were found the next morning. Father Fuster reported of the body, "There was not a sound spot on it except for his innocent hands." Father Fuster buried his pastor's remains in the presidio chapel, and later they were transferred to the reconstructed mission. They rest today in the restored mission church, and the site of the martyrdom is marked by a cross. Conversion increased rapidly after the martyrdom, proving Father Serra's prophecy and illustrating once again the adage, "The blood of martyrs is the seed of Christianity."

Sources:
CCCMUS
Geiger, M., *Franciscan Missionaries in Spanish America*
Habig, Marion, *Heroes of the Cross*
Cicognani, A.G., *Sanctity in America*

111. Father Juan Marcello Díaz, Franciscan (1781)
112. Father José Matías Moreno, Franciscan
113. Father Francisco Hermenegildo Garcés, Franciscan
114. Father Juan Antonio Barreneche, Franciscan

In establishing their California missions, the Franciscans followed the Jesuit system of reductions. That is, they removed their permanent missions from the vicinity of Spanish settlements and presidios. They realized that Spanish soldiers and settlers did not always give good example, in many cases abusing the Indians and trying to make serfs of them. The Franciscans built their own self-sufficient worlds in their attempt to create ideal situations in which new converts might live and grow in their new faith.

However, when new missions were to be established among the Yuma Indians in southeastern California along the Colorado River, the Spanish *comandante* ruled that the missions must be part of the Spanish settlements, that the Indians must live side by side with the colonists, and that the missioners would confine themselves to ritual — preaching, saying Mass, and administering the sacraments. The Franciscans protested to no avail. The result was what they had feared. The Spaniards moved in on Indian lands and abused the native inhabitants. The Indians in turn developed a hatred for the intruders and their religion. This acrimony came to a head when the *comandante* arrested an Indian chief (Palma) and placed him in stocks. The Indians rose in a rebellion that took the lives of the four priests listed above.

Fathers Juan Díaz and José Moreno were stationed at Misión San Pedro y San Pablo de Bicuner, which was located on the Colorado about three miles north of Fort Yuma. Father Díaz had been born in Alcázar de San Juan, Seville, Spain, in 1736. He entered the Franciscans at eighteen and after ordination volunteered for the American missions, arriving in Mexico in 1763. After the Jesuits had been expelled from their missions, he went to work among the Pima Indians, where he had considerable success in conversions. He was one of a small group of Spaniards who pioneered an overland route from Mexico to San Diego. He began the Misión San Pedro y San Pablo, full of misgivings at the newly imposed system of colonization. Father Moreno, born in Almorza, Spain, joined the Franciscans in Burgos in 1762. He was assigned to the Franciscan missionary college at Querétaro, Mexico, and from there to Sonora. When the missions among the Yumas was established, he was chosen to assist Father Díaz.

The other two murdered Franciscans were stationed at Misión Purisima Concepción. Father Francisco Garcés was an extraordinary missioner who has been compared to the great Jesuit missioner Father Kino. He was born in Aragón, Spain, in 1738, and received his early education from an uncle who was a priest. He entered the Franciscans at the age of fifteen and was ordained ten years later. He volunteered for the Indian missions and arrived at Queretaro in 1766, serving for a time as a confessor. He was assigned to the now famous mission of San Xavier del Bac, near Tucson, where he won a reputation for his spiritual ministrations and his explorations in uncharted areas of California and Arizona. In 1768 he traveled among the tribes along the Gila River, and the following year he entered the country of the Apaches.

In 1771 he followed the Colorado River to its mouth. He was the first to reach the Grand Canyon from the west and the first to give it a specific name, other than the name of the river flowing through it. The historian Herbert E. Bolton has called Garcés "intrepid," "heroic," and "fearless." However, not all was exploration. When he learned that an epidemic had broken out in the Gila region, he hastened there, baptizing as many dying children as he could. He chronicled his journeys — more than 5,000 miles by foot —

and sent the reports on to the authorities. On one of his journeys (one of eleven months), he had made friends with the Yuman Indians, and Chief Palma, who would later be put in stocks, asked for missioners. When it was decided that settlements should be made among the Yumas, it was natural that he should be chosen to lead the Franciscans.

With Father Garcés at Purisima Concepción was Father Barreneche, a Navarrese Spaniard, born in 1749. Barreneche had gone in the employ of a merchant of Havana, Cuba, as a teenager. When he was nineteen, he joined the Franciscans in Havana and was sent to the college in Querétaro for his studies. Ordained there around 1776, a man of deep religious spirit and entirely unworldly, he was chosen to assist Father Garcés in working among the Yumas. In a letter back to Mexico, Father Garcés highly praised the zeal of his confrere, referring to him as "another St. Patrick."

The revolt by the Yumas against the Spaniards began on July 19, 1781. Fathers Díaz and Moreno died on that day, beaten to death by clubs. When the bodies were recovered five months later, evidence pointed to the fact that Father Moreno had also been decapitated. Fathers Garcés and Barreneche survived the first two days, hearing the confessions of dying Spaniards. They took refuge among some Christian Indians, and Chief Palma had put out the word that they were not to be harmed. However, on the morning of July 19, they were discovered by a pagan Indian who summoned others, and they were beaten to death. When the bodies of all four men were recovered, they were moved to the Querétaro college for final burial.

Sources:
CCCMUS
Geiger, M., *Franciscan Missionaries in Spanish America*
Habig, Marion, *Heroes of the Cross*
Lesser Brothers, Quarterly Chronicle, Franciscan Province of the

Sacred Heart (January 1972), "White Dove of the Desert" by Marion A. Habig.

115. Father Andrés Quintana, Franciscan (1812)

Father Andrés Quintana was born in Antonorro, Spain, in 1777. He entered the Franciscan order at the age of seventeen in the province of Cantabria, where he was ordained. On April 26, 1804, he set sail from Cádiz for Mexico, where he volunteered for the California missions. Arriving at Monterey at the end of August the following year, he was assigned to Santa Cruz, where he was to labor until his death in 1812, although he occasionally helped out at San Juan Bautista when the resident priest was away.

On October 12, 1812, he was found dead in his bed. Since he had been ill, his death was attributed to natural causes and he was buried. About two years later some Indians were heard speaking about Quintana being murdered. This was reported to the authorities and an investigation was made. Eight Indians were arrested. They admitted their guilt, saying that the priest had been harsh with them. During the night, they had feigned a sick call, and Father Quintana, though ill himself, answered it. Once away from the mission, they killed him "in a most revolting and diabolical manner." After the priest was dead, they brought him back and laid him in his bed. The body was exhumed and examined by a surgeon and the murder established. A fellow missioner, Father Narciso Duran, in writing to his superior in 1814, declared that the Indians "murdered him in so barbarous a manner that I doubt if such cruelty has even been resorted to in the most barbarous nations, for they tortured him *in pudentis* and suffocated him at the same time."

Governor Pablo Sola conducted a careful inquiry of the

matter and wrote that, instead of being harsh, "this good Father went to excess, not in punishing his Indians but in the love with which he regarded them." He called Father Quintana "a very pious missioner" who, while seriously ill himself, responded to the call of ministry "which was the cause of his premature death." The governor referred the case to the viceroy, and the murderers were punished with imprisonment. Years later, an English writer, Sir George Simpson, accused Father Quintana of immorality in his narrative and gave that as the reason for his death. However, this is put down as unfounded gossip and was never claimed by the Indian murderers in their defense at the trial.

Sources:
CCCMUS
Greiger, M., *Franciscan Missionaries in Spanish America*
Habig, Marion, *Heroes of the Cross*

Texas

116. Father Antonio Díaz de León, Franciscan (1834)

Father Díaz has been called the "Last Padre of Texas." He was the superior of the Texas missions when they were secularized and their land divided between Indians and settlers. The Spanish padres were forced to return to Spain, and there were not sufficient Mexican padres to make up their loss. Along with the others. Father Díaz returned to Mexico. In 1832, however, the Bishop of Monterey asked him to minister to the needs of scattered Catholics in the vicinity of Nacogdoches in eastern Texas. The new responsibility made him a traveling missioner, as he moved from settlement to settlement seeking out those whom he could serve. The area was filled with newcomers, some of them bandits who had fled to Texas because they were wanted in the United States, others ruffians and roustabouts looking for opportunities for gain, still others bigots against the Catholic Church and its priests. Some of these latter made threats against Father Díaz, but he could not imagine anyone doing him injury.

Father Díaz had considerable success. He brought many Catholics back to their religion and converted other Anglos. In 1833 he baptized Sam Houston, who was to win independence for Texas at the Battle of San Jacinto three years later. When in late October 1834 he was asked to go to the Trinity River to witness a marriage, he hesitated because threats against him had become so insistent. Duty seemed more important, however, so he went and after the wedding visited Catholics in the vicinity, accompanied by a Kentuckian, Philip Miller, whom the groom had sent along to protect the priest.

On November 2, he was at the home of Peter Menard, a Catholic, when he had a premonition of death. With paper and ink borrowed from his host, he wrote a last will and testament, stating in it that "it seems to me to be the last day of my life — God knows why." They stopped at another farm the next day and on November 3 traveled about twenty miles to Big Sandy Creek, where they made camp for the night. Shortly before daybreak, Miller later reported, he was awakened by something, but not a shot. He went to stir up the fire and found Father Díaz with blood trickling from his mouth, a pistol "near the body," instantly killed by a shot through the heart. What happened that night was never determined. Whether Miller killed the priest or covered up for some enemy who crept up in the night, no one ever found out. It was the opinion of Catholics that the zealous priest had been the victim of one of the bigots who had threatened him. The Catholics believed he was killed for his Faith and was a martyr. The death took place near San Augustine, thirty miles from Nacogdoches, on November 4. He was buried by Miller and a settler, and the grave has never been found.

Sources:
CCCMUS
Habig, Marion, *Heroes of the Cross*
                San Antonio's Mission San José (Chapter X)

California

117. Father Francis Bassost, Capuchin (1872)

Father Bassost, a Spanish missioner, established the Capuchin missions in Guatemala, where he was superior. In 1872 the anticlerical revolutionary government expelled all foreign missioners from Guatemala. Father Bassost was arrested along with thirty-eight other Capuchins in the region of Antigua, the old capital. They were forced to journey two hundred miles to the coast, where, on June 16, they were put aboard a ship bound for San Francisco. Father Bassost had fallen ill from the hardships he had to endure during the expulsion. The ship reached San Francisco on July 1, and Father Bassost went ashore. He died three days later (July 4) from the cruel effects of his banishment. Since he died in San Francisco, he is considered a martyr of the United States.

Sources:
CCCMUS
Habig, Marion, *Heroes of the Cross*
Cambrils, Ignatius, *Chronicle of the Missions of the Capuchin Fathers in Central America*

105

118. Archbishop Charles J. Seghers (1886)
Protomartyr of Alaska

Charles John Seghers was born in Ghent, Belgium, December 26, 1839. His parents died while he was still a young boy, and he was raised by relatives. He studied in Ghent and at the American College of Louvain. Ordained May 31, 1863, he responded to a missionary call from Bishop Demers of Victoria, Canada, arriving on Vancouver Island, November 19, 1863. At that time Victoria was a suffragan see of the Archdiocese of Oregon City in the United States. That vicariate had been established in 1845, and Francis Norbert Blanchet was appointed first Vicar Apostolic of the Oregon Territory. A year later the area was raised to a province, and Blanchet was named archbishop.

Father Seghers was assigned to the cathedral in Victoria and soon became the right hand of Bishop Demers, who wrote to a friend, "My dear Seghers is the idol of everyone." When Bishop Demers was away, Father Seghers acted as administrator of the diocese. On June 29, 1873, Father Seghers was consecrated Bishop of Victoria, succeeding his mentor, who had died some eighteen months earlier. The new bishop immediately made a long journey into Alaska to become acquainted with his territory. Returning from another exhausting tour of the north in 1878, during which he visited thirty thousand Indians, he learned that he had been named coadjutor to Archbishop Blanchet in Oregon City (now the Archdiocese of Portland).

Two years later, when Archbishop Blanchet resigned his see, Seghers was named to replace him (December 20, 1880). The new archbishop again took up the arduous travels of his region, the Oregon missions and the Vicariate of Idaho. While he was in Rome for the Plenary Council of Baltimore, his own see of Victoria became vacant and the head of the

Archbishop Charles J. Seghers, martyred in Alaska, 1886

Congregation for the Propagation of the Faith (Propaganda) consulted him about who should succeed to Victoria. The cardinal stressed that the person chosen had to be concerned for Alaska, where no work was being done.

"Your Eminence," Archbishop Seghers is said to have replied, "let me go back to Victoria, and I shall take care of Alaska."

Cardinal Simone conferred with Pope Leo XIII, and it was decided that Archbishop Seghers could resign Oregon and return to Victoria. This took place in 1884. He obtained the aid of Jesuits from the Rocky Mountain Province in the United States, whom he had met while visiting Idaho. He also established permanent missions in Juneau and Sitka to care for Indians and Eskimos.

In 1886 Archbishop Seghers began his fifth and final journey through Alaska. He had gained the enmity of white traders who saw the development of missions among the Indians as putting an end to their exploitation. Some of the more bitterly anti-Catholic whites were particularly incensed over the coming of the Jesuits to the region. On this journey, the archbishop left two Jesuits at Harper's Place at the mouth of the Stewart River to begin work among the Indians. With a guide, Francis Fuller, who had worked with the Jesuits in Coeur d'Alene, and two Indians, the Archbishop set out down the Yukon for Nulato. The journey was difficult, and they finally made camp at a place called Nuklukayet, where they found two prospectors and a trader named Walker who had holed up there against the coming winter. Archbishop Seghers decided to wait at Nuklukayet until the Yukon was frozen solid and then follow it to Nulato.

After some weeks, the party set out again by dogsled. By this time Fuller was beginning to act strangely, saying that the archbishop would destroy them all on this terrible journey. He had also picked up some anti-mission ideas from the fur trader at Nuklukayet, who had told him that the bishop was "dangerous," and "an enemy." He was still sulking when, a day or two from Nulato, the group camped for the night in an abandoned hut used by fishermen during the salmon run. Toward morning, Fuller arose and without any warning shot the archbishop through the heart, killing him instantly. The date was either November 17 or November 28, 1886, as nearly as could be determined by the Indians' testimony.

It was six months before the news of the archbishop's death reached Alaskan civilization. Fuller was arrested, found guilty of manslaughter, and sent to prison. Years later when he was released, he himself was shot to death near Portland. The trader Walker, who many believe was really behind the killing by persuading the already disturbed mind of Fuller that the archbishop was evil, died in 1891 of delirium tremens. The body of the archbishop was recovered and entombed under the high altar of the cathedral in Victoria, British Columbia. In 1894 the Jesuits were given care of the Vicariate Apostolic of Alaska.

Sources:
CCCMUS
Catholic Encyclopedia
Bosco, Antoinette, *Charles John Seghers, Pioneer in Alaska*
Habig, Marion, *Heroes of the Cross*

Colorado

119. Father Leo Heinrich, Franciscan (1908)
Protomartyr of Colorado

Father Leo Heinrich was born in Oesterich of the Archdiocese of Cologne, Germany, on August 5, 1867. As a boy he expressed the desire to become a Franciscan, and because Bismarck's May Law required all youths to spend three years in the German army, he was sent to the Franciscan Monastery in Paterson, New Jersey. Here he completed his studies and was ordained a priest on July 26, 1891.

In the years that followed, Father Heinrich worked in various parishes in New Jersey and New York and served as director of the Franciscan Third Order. As pastor of St. Stephen's Parish in Groghan, New York, he rebuilt the church and school after the original buildings had been destroyed by fire. He was known for his kindliness, cheer, and charity. Unknown to the people he served, he practiced many mortifications and penances and wore a barbed steel belt next to his flesh. In 1907 he was named pastor of St. Elizabeth's Parish in Denver, Colorado.

In Denver, Father Heinrich again won friends by his kindliness. He made a special apostolate of concern for the poor, feeding hungry men, women, and children every morning, and giving them clothing when it was needed. One Saturday evening, he heard confessions until eleven o'clock at night. Because he wanted to attend a meeting the next day, he asked to take the 6:00 A.M. Sunday Mass, which had been assigned to another priest.

Thus on Sunday, February 23, 1908, Father Heinrich said the early parish Mass. Nothing untoward happened until the priest was distributing Holy Communion. As he went along the altar rail, he came to a man who received the Host in the ordinary manner. Then a series of events transpired faster than can be written down here. Without warning, the man spit out the Host, reached inside his coat, and pulled out a gun. The altar boy, Joseph Hines, saw the weapon and cried out to Father Heinrich. But before the priest could react, the man fired a bullet through the Franciscan's heart. As the priest sank to the floor of the sanctuary, he reached out to set down the ciborium on the step of the Lady's Altar, but a few Hosts spilled to the floor. Father Heinrich died pointing to the fallen Hosts, his last thought being the sanctity of the Blessed Sacrament.

The assassin made for the exit of the church, but a policeman, David Cronin, at Mass before going on duty, caught and disarmed him. The murderer, Giuseppe Alia, was a 56-year-old Sicilian, a shoemaker by trade, a Socialist and anarchist. He had come to America two years earlier to spread the teachings of anarchism among Italians. He had worked in New Jersey, in Massachusetts, and around Chicago, preaching his doctrine in mill towns. He had no remorse for his act, which he said was done out of hatred of the Church. He had seated himself in front of the pulpit and intended to shoot the priest while he preached. However, no sermon was given at the first Mass on Sunday so that people could get to work. So he revised his plan to Communion time. He also said that if he had not been arrested, he had planned to kill three more priests. After his arrest, the police had to secrete him in several prisons to avoid lynching. He was ultimately convicted of the crime and executed.

Father Heinrich's funeral was the largest Denver had ever seen. The church was packed with mourners, among them the Governor of Colorado and the Mayor of Denver. Thousands more jammed the streets outside. A long procession made its way after the funeral Mass to Union Station, and the body was placed aboard a train for Paterson, N.J., where it was interred in the monastery cemetery.

Sources:
The Denver Catholic Register, February 28, 1908
The Denver Catholic Register, March 3, 1927
Archives, Archdiocese of Denver
Habig, Marion, *Heroes of the Cross*

Alabama

120. Father James Edwin Coyle (1921)

In the 1920s there was an upsurge of membership in and power of the Ku Klux Klan in the South. Catholics, Jews, and Negroes were assailed and discriminated against, and in some towns it was even dangerous for a minority member to be alone on the street. Beatings and lynchings were not rare, and justice was selective in its rendering. It was in such an atmosphere that Father James Edwin Coyle was murdered and his death went unpunished.

Father Coyle was born in Ireland on March 23, 1873. He received his Bachelor of Arts degree from Mungret Apostolic College there and undertook his theological studies at the North American College in Rome, where he was ordained for the Diocese of Mobile (Alabama) in 1896. He was first assigned to the Cathedral parish in Mobile, and in 1898 he became president of McGill Institute, a high school. In 1904 he was named to the important pastorate and deanery of St. Paul's, Birmingham. He was a member of the diocesan council, chaplain of the Knights of Columbus and a number of other societies, and editor of the Catholic monthly.

All who knew Father Coyle praised him as an exemplary priest. One who was baptized by him later wrote: "We all loved and revered Father Coyle. He was a very pious, kindly, saintly man." Because he was an outstanding Catholic and civic leader, he incurred the enmity of the Ku Klux Klan, which had secured control of the government and courts in Birmingham. He defended Catholicism and replied to anti-Irish attacks both in his own paper and in the Birmingham dailies, and although his responses were always temperate and scholarly, they did bring threats to his life. An offshoot of the Klan in Birmingham was a secret group known as "True Americans." Its members were noted for flogging whites who associated with blacks. It had for a motto "No Catholics in public office." As a result, Catholics were not hired for city jobs and vigilance committees threatened boycotts of merchants who employed Catholics. Its members were to promote sympathy for Father Coyle's murderer.

It was in this atmosphere that Father Coyle witnessed the marriage of Ruth Stephenson and Pedro Gussman on April 11, 1921. Miss Stephenson, a recent convert to the Catholic Church, was the daughter of Edwin R. Stephenson, an ignorant itinerant Methodist preacher and a member of the Klan. Mr. Stephenson had no parish but frequented the courthouse to perform weddings and thus became known as the "Marrying Preacher." Mr. Gussman was Puerto Rican. The Catholic wedding incensed Mr. Stephenson, and edged on by cohorts at the court house, he went to Father Coyle's rectory an hour after the wedding. He found the priest sitting in a rocker on the porch, reciting the Divine Office. He drew a gun and fired one shot into Father Coyle's head. Then he went and surrendered to the police. Father Coyle was rushed to the hospital and died there within an hour. He was buried with a Pontifical Requiem Mass on August 14 and interred in Our Lady of Sorrows Cemetery. In 1937 the remains were moved to Elmwood Cemetery.

On October 17, 1921, the widely publicized Stephenson trial opened. The preacher was defended by a Birmingham attorney, Hugo Black, a member of the Klan and later a United States Supreme Court Justice. The judge, William E. Fort, was another Klansman, as were most of the jury. The Black defense was one of temporary insanity. The State produced only five witnesses who testified to the shooting (which Stephenson admitted) but refused to call Ruth Gussman. Black argued that the father was temporarily deranged over the "prosyletism" of his daughter (another priest, not Father Coyle, had received the girl into the Church). He attempted to introduce bigotry into the trial by attacking the Spanish ancestry of Gussman, declaring that Puerto Ricans were largely mulattos. He had Gussman brought into the court to stand before the jury without testifying, having first drawn the blinds so that the man would appear darker, declaring that if Gussman was "of proud

Castilian descent, he has descended a long way." Rebutting the defense, he attacked two of the state's Catholic eyewitnesses as glaringly inaccurate and "brothers in falsehood as also in faith." The jury took one ballot and found the minister not guilty. The *Birmingham News* denounced the verdict the next day, and unbiased witnesses accused Black of appealing to prejudice.

The murder and trial had echoes sixteen years later when Hugo Black, nominated by Franklin D. Roosevelt to the Supreme Court, was before the United States Senate for confirmation hearings. Senator Royal S. Copeland of New York, who opposed the nomination, offered to bring Judge Fort before the Senate to testify that both he and Black had been Klansmen at the time of the trial. Black produced a copy of a letter he wrote in 1925 to the Alabama Grand Dragon, resigning from the Klan. The matter was not pursued, and Black was confirmed.

Sources:

Lovett, Rose Gibbons, *Centennial History of St. Paul's Parish* (Unpublished)

Hamilton, Virginia Van der Veer, *Hugo Black*

Snell, William Robert, *The Ku Klux Klan in Jefferson County* (Unpublished thesis, Birmingham Public Library)

Lovett, Rose Gibbons, private correspondence to the author

Jefferson County Department of Health, death certificate of Father Coyle

Birmingham Age-Herald, October 18, 22, 1921

The New York Times, August 12, 1921; October 22, 1921

Birmingham News, October 17, 1921

California

121. Father Patrick E. Heslin (1921)

Father Patrick E. Heslin was killed simply because he was a priest. Father Heslin was attached to the Archdiocese of San Francisco and was the brother of Bishop Thomas Heslin, who had been Bishop of Natchez, Mississippi, from 1899 to 1911. He had previously been stationed at Turlock and had been at Holy Angels Parish in Colma only two weeks before his death.

On the evening of August 2, 1921, a seedy-looking man approached Father Heslin and asked if a priest could go with him to a friend who was dying. Father Heslin went with the man and was never seen alive again.

Archbishop Edward Hanna, head of the San Francisco Archdiocese, received a letter demanding that he bring ransom for Father Heslin, and warning the archbishop not to be accompanied by any "damn knights" (Knights of Columbus) and not to make the letter public, as it would be "easy to trap you bunch of imposters."

Several days later, Father Heslin's body was found in a shallow grave on a beach at San Mateo. The man who led the police to the body, William Hightower, was arrested and convicted of the murder. The police considered the crime an act of anti-Catholic violence. There was no legitimate sick call, and Father Heslin was killed because he exercised his priestly ministry.

Sources:
The Catholic Week (Birmingham), October 31, 1941
Chancery Archives, Archdiocese of San Francisco

China

122. Father Walter Coveyou, Passionist (1929)
123. Father Clement Seybold, Passionist
124. Father Godfrey Holbein, Passionist
First American Martyrs Outside the United States

Although the Chinese Communists did not come to power until after World War II, bands of Reds were active in the country decades earlier. Catholic missions were a frequent target for those enemies of religion, and it was a Red band that put to death the first American Catholics to be martyred outside their own country. These were three priests of the Congregation of the Passion (Passionists) from the Province of St. Paul of the Cross, then headquartered in Union City, N.J.

Father Walter Coveyou, C.P., was born in Petosky, Michigan, on October 17, 1894. He was received into the Passionist Order in 1912 and was ordained May 29, 1920. Although early in his priesthood he volunteered for foreign mission work, his superiors did not send him abroad until September 1928. He was hardly six months in China when he was murdered.

Father Clement Seybold was born in Dunkirk, New York, on April 18, 1896, receiving his primary education there in St. Mary's School. He was professed as a Passionist on September 17, 1918, and ordained October 28, 1923. While yet a student, he asked to be assigned to the missions, a wish that was granted after ordination. In July, 1924, he sailed for China.

Father Godfrey Holbein was born in Baltimore on February 4, 1899. After graduating from St. Joseph's Parochial School there, he entered Holy Cross College in Dunkirk, New York, to become a Passionist, making his profession on May 16, 1917. He was ordained October 28, 1923. Father Godfrey also volunteered for China, in fact begging his superiors to send him there. He had frequently told friends that he longed for martyrdom and that China seemed to offer the greatest opportunity toward that end. He sailed for China in July 1924, and, like the others, he spent his first year learning Chinese. When he was assigned to an outlying mission station, he had to flee because of the chaos caused by the Red Revolution. From the safety of Hankow he wrote, "I would return tomorrow if it were at all possible. And if our other Fathers and our Sisters are killed I think I shall lose my mind." He opined that in the sight of God such deaths would be martyrdom, and he concluded, "And to think that I have missed the one big opportunity that I might have had!"

The Passionist Mission in China was in the southwest quadrant of Hunan Province. It was an area that had been wracked by civil war. However, early in 1929 the government troops had regained control and the fighting had ended. There were, nevertheless, pockets of Red soldiers who had turned to banditry, exacting tribute whenever the occasion arose. In the second week of April, Fathers Walter, Clement, and Godfrey had gone to Shenchau for their annual retreat. On Sunday, April 21, after morning Mass, the three missioners left for Yuanchau to replace three other Passionists in the area so that they could make a retreat. The journey had to be made on foot and muleback through mountainous terrain. The priests were accompanied by several mission employees acting as guides, interpreters, and baggage carriers.

Late on Tuesday afternoon, the party reached the market village of Hwa Chiao, where they arranged lodging for the night at an inn. After dark, two armed men entered the inn, questioned the priests, and examined their baggage. The missioners presumed that they belonged to the home guard. Later, when an investigation was made, it was determined that they were bandits and that the inn owner was in league with them, perhaps out of fear, perhaps from conviction. (The inn owner was later executed by the military for her part in the murders.)

Early the next morning, assured that there were no bandits around, the priests nevertheless wanted to start quickly for Hwa Chiao, where they knew soldiers were stationed. The missioners had not even gone half a mile beyond the village when they were surrounded by sixteen or seventeen bandits, who led them off the path, back into the mountains. After covering some distance, the priests were ordered up a hill where there was an abandoned copper mine. Two mission altar boys, Peter and Cosmas, went with them. Father Godfrey told the boys to say an Act of Contrition and he gave them absolution. At the top of the hill, the bandits ordered the priests to strip. Father Walter, new to China and not familiar with the dialect, said in Chinese, "I don't understand you." The bandit who had given the order immediately fired a shot into the priest's head. The body collapsed into the grass. Father Clement, who was stooped, untying his shoes, was then shot in the head, the bullet almost tearing his head in two. Peter noticed Father Clement, his hand raised as if in blessing, as the bandit swung and fired two shots into the surviving missioner.

The two boys and the porters were set free by the bandits after being warned not to work for "foreign devils." They made their way to safety and reported the murders. They also said that the man who did the killing was the one who had been at the inn the night before, questioning the priests. Their testimony implicated the inn owner and several in the home guard as assisting the bandits.

A search was made for the bodies, and they were discovered at the bottom of the abandoned mine shaft. They were recovered and taken to Shenchau for funeral ceremonies and burial. The military ruled that the priests were killed by Communist bandits in hatred of the "foreign religion." It was pointed out that no ransom was planned, but instead the victims were taken to a prearranged spot, where they could be killed and their bodies supposedly hidden in the deep pit. The murders were planned and were not by accident. The hatred was against the priests and not their Chinese assistants. The date of the martyrdom was April 24, 1929.

As an interesting sidelight to the martyrdoms, a nephew of Father Godfrey was inspired by his uncle's death to become a missioner himself. He joined the Maryknoll Fathers and in time was also sent to China, where he worked in a leper colony until the Chinese Communists arrested him and forced him out of the country. He is presently a missioner in Central America, where again he is threatened by Communists.

Sources:
The Sign, June 1929
The Sign, July 1929
The Field Afar, June 1929

Manchuria (China)

125. Father Gerard A. Donovan, Maryknoll (1928)

Father Gerard A. Donovan, M.M., of Pittsburgh, Pennsylvania, was born October 14, 1904. He followed two older brothers into the Catholic Foreign Mission Society of America (Maryknoll) to prepare for overseas mission work. He was ordained at Maryknoll, New York, on June 17, 1928, and appointed to the Manchurian mission field. Manchuria, formerly a part of China, was then under Japanese occupation. After learning the language, he was assigned to various parishes and responsibilities.

On the evening of October 5, 1937, Father Donovan was kneeling at Benediction in the sanctuary of the Hopei mission church when a man entered the sacristy and called him out. Thinking that there was some emergency, Father Donovan went into the sacristy where the man drew a gun and ordered the priest to accompany him. At that moment an unsuspecting altar boy, Francis Liu, entered the sacristy for the censer and was also taken prisoner. The man hurried thepriest and altar boy outside, and they disappeared into the growing dusk.

Almost immediately the alarm was given, and the Japanese authorities were notified, but no trace of the missing priest was found. Two weeks later a weary Francis Liu returned to the mission. He had been released by his captors with a note demanding $50,000 ransom for the priest. Since many of the Maryknoll missions in China and Manchuria were plagued by bandits, the Society had adopted a policy of paying no ransom demands, knowing that if it ransomed the priest, no other missioner would be safe. Some months earlier another Maryknoll priest had been kidnapped, but after ransom was refused, he was freed.

Francis Liu told what had happened. As soon as Father Donovan and the altar boy were clear of the mission, their hands were bound. Other bandits joined the group, and they traveled all that night and for the next ten nights, hiding and sleeping in the hills by day. Eventually, they reached a camp where the only shelter was a large lean-to with a roof but no walls. The nights were cold, and priest and boy covered themselves with grass and weeds to keep warm. The bandits took the priest's trousers and shoes, giving him a pair of cotton trousers and sneakers in return. Francis said that they threatened Father Donovan with death, but he told them, "Do as you please. The Church has no money for ransom."

"He was always in good spirits," Francis reported. "We talked a lot, and he was always trying to give me courage because I was afraid. Father would smile at me and say, 'Don't worry. There's nothing to be afraid of. They'll let you go home soon. Pray hard.' "

Although the Japanese sent soldiers into the area indicated by the altar boy, the search turned up nothing. Weeks and months passed by with no clue to the missioner's whereabouts. Then on February 11, 1938, Japanese soldiers came across Father Donovan's frozen body on a mountainside, a rope garrote around his neck. In his hand he clutched the bottom of his cincture with its distinctive chi-rho insignia. He had evidently cut it off and hidden it in his hand as a means of identification.

The United States Consulate at Mukden sent the following wire to the Maryknoll superior: "(Consul) Ludden and Father Thomas Quirk of Catholic Church report positive identification of the body discovered by military authorities as that of Gerard Donovan. Difficult to determine exact time of death, but it is believed Father Donovan died one week before the discovery of the remains. Emaciated condition of the scantily clad body indicates extreme hardships suffered during captivity. Body partially eaten by wolves. Military authorities state there are no gunshot wounds and attribute death to strangulation."

The remains were returned to the mission center for funeral rites and then transferred to Maryknoll, New York, for burial. It is the policy of the Maryknoll Society to bury its priests where they die, but because Father Donovan was the first Maryknoller to die violently, an exception was made in the belief that even in death he could be an inspiration to American youth.

Sources:
Considine, John J., *When the Sorghum Was High*
Berger, Meyer, *Men of Maryknoll*
Nevins, Albert J., *The Meaning of Maryknoll*

China

126. Father Robert J. Cairns, Maryknoll (1941)

Among the earliest American missioners in China was Father Robert J. Cairns of Worcester, Massachusetts. Father Cairns was born in Worcester, August 21, 1884. He joined the newly-founded Maryknoll Society from Holy Cross College and was ordained May 18, 1918. Maryknoll decided to open a "procure" in Kowloon (Hong Kong) in 1920 that would serve the missioners who were beginning work in the area of Yeungkong, China. The house would give Maryknoll a presence in Hong Kong and would purchase and ship supplies to the men upcountry and serve as a rest house for missioners. Father Cairns was placed in charge. When Maryknoll was given its first mission territory of Kongmoon, Father Cairns became a part of that mission.

Known to his friends as Father Sandy because of his Scottish heritage, he made every effort to identify himself with the Chinese people and was successful in making converts. During a period of famine he did heroic work providing relief food for the needy. Part of the new Kongmoon Mission was Sancian Island, a sacred place because it was the spot where St. Francis Xavier had died while trying to get into China, then The Forbidden Kingdom. A shrine had been built there in the saint's memory, marking his first burial place. In 1933 Father Cairns was put in charge. He promoted the shrine and took care of the island's Christians, being successful at both efforts. Many pilgrims began coming to Sancian, and the Church there was growing.

A few days after Pearl Harbor, a Japanese boat put into Sancian and Father Cairns was warned to leave. "Otherwise you will be killed," he was told.

"I expect so," replied the priest, determined that he was not going to be forced away from his people.

Some days later the Japanese returned. Armed soldiers went ashore, made directly for the mission, and arrested Father Cairns, then looted shops and burned a village. The exact date is unknown, but island witnesses saw the bound priest forced aboard the enemy vessel. Some Chinese on the island said that Father Cairns was put in a pig basket (a contraption used to take pigs to market), loaded aboard the boat and then thrown into the South China Sea. Another report said he was taken aboard the boat, shot and then thrown overboard. Actually, the two stories do not necessarily conflict. The best date for his death is December 1941.

Sources:
Nevins, Albert J., *The Meaning of Maryknoll*
Maryknoll Archives
Miller, Ed Mack, *Maryknoll at Work in the World*

Solomon Islands

127. Father Arthur C. Duhamel, Marist (1942)

Following Pearl Harbor and the outbreak of the Pacific
War, the Japanese in their advance on Australia occupied
various Pacific Islands. Many of these islands were missions
of the Marist Fathers, who specialized in the conversion of
Oceania. A number of these missioners were killed by invading troops, among them Father Arthur C. Duhamel, a
Marist from Methuen, Massachusetts. That Father
Duhamel's death was caused more by hatred for his religion
than his Americanism is shown in the fact that a Dutch
priest and two French Sisters were murdered with him, and
in the disrespect shown for the mission itself.

Arthur Duhamel, one of eleven children of François and
Marie Duhamel, was born in Lawrence, Massachusetts, on
October 19, 1908. When he was ten, the family moved to
Methuen, where he graduated from Mt. Carmel School.
Then, at the age of fourteen, he went to work in a woolen
factory, attending night school to continue his education.
When he was sixteen, he applied to and was accepted by the
Marist Fathers, making his profession in that congregation
in 1931. He completed his studies at the Marist Seminary,
Washington, D.C., where he was ordained June 15, 1937.
For the next two years he assisted in a Marist parish in Van
Buren, Maine, where he also taught religion.

In 1939 he was assigned to the Solomon Islands and was
stationed at Ruavatu, Guadalcanal, with other Marists. He
busied himself in learning the language of the people, which

he found difficult. He also learned that mission work was more than the teaching of religion. There were arduous mountain journeys to distant villages and trips by boat along the coast. The natives discovered that he had a mechanical talent for fixing clocks, and they were continuously bringing old timepieces to him. He also had to tend the mission farm that supplied vegetables, and to do such odd jobs as painting the Sisters' convent, but despite the manual labor, his letters home told of his happiness.

When war broke out in the Pacific, it seemed to have passed by Guadalcanal. His letters stated that as yet there was no cause to worry, adding, "I saw a Japanese plane once or twice from a distance, but that is all." Instead, he dwelt on his mission work. In one of his last letters he wrote, "The work is difficult here because of the rough mountainous country and the dangerous rivers on which we must use a launch to travel. Fever comes all too often, dulling the senses, but when we work for God difficulties become sweet. My one desire is that God will give me health and the necessary means to keep on marching ahead for the salvation of these poor Solomonese, among whom His Providence has called me to work."

The idyll, however, was not to continue. The Japanese did land on the island and began to build defenses. In time, too, they came to Ruavatu. Details are sparse, but two Solomonese boys who were with the missionaries gave some details. When it seemed that Japanese invasion was imminent, the priests encouraged their people to retreat to the hills, but they themselves refused to leave because they wanted to protect the mission property. Yet there was little protection they could give when the attack came without warning. The two priests, Father Duhamel and Father Henry Engerbrink, from Utrecht, Netherlands, and two French Sisters, Sister Odilla and Mary Sylvia, the latter a thirty-year veteran, were seized. The soldiers led the missioners to the beach. Perhaps the first intention was to take them to a jail, but an order was given and they were all bayoneted to death. Father Duhamel died as he was giving a last blessing to his companions. The Japanese then pillaged the mission, trampling sacred objects underfoot and shredding vestments. After they left, Christian natives buried the bodies of the slain missioners by an abandoned house near the beach. The date of the massacre was September 14, 1942.

In time, after a fierce battle, the American Marines reconquered Guadalcanal, and as normalcy was restored, a native chief told the Americans of the death of their missioners. General Lawton Collins asked Chaplain T.P. Finnegan to look into the matter. The chief led Father Finnegan and a detail of Marines to the graves. The bodies were exhumed, identified, and reburied in front of the Ruavatu Mission, the priests on the Gospel side and the Sisters on the Epistle side. General Collins also ordered that the mission be restored. In his report, Father Finnegan told how he found the mission full of wreckage: "Every religious article and all personal mementoes were wantonly torn, to be cast in shreds on the floor. . . . The once beautiful chapel was especially discouraging; torn vestments and broken statues were scattered about the floor. . . . The vessels for the sacred oils had been crushed underfoot before the altar. Needless to say, we cleaned the chapel very depressed in spirits."

One bright spot turned up. When the natives learned that the chaplain was a priest, they led him miles into the jungle, where hidden in the forest they had built a thatch chapel to St. Michael, and in it they had the large mission tabernacle rescued from the ruined mission church. Father Finnegan spent the weekend among these people, saying Mass, hearing confessions, and being greatly moved by the faith of the people for whom the missioners had given their lives.

Sources:
Private papers, Mr. Lionel Duhamel, Meuthen, Masssachusetts

(Author's Note. Two names are given for one of the Sisters who died with Father Duhamel. Father Finnegan's report gives it as Sister Mary Sylvia, which is found elsewhere. Other accounts list her as Sister Mary Salome.)

Solomon Islands

128. Father James Gerard Hennessey (1942)

One of the tragedies of World War II was that a considerable number of American lives were ended by action of their own military forces when American submarines sank Japanese ships carrying Allied prisoners of war. One who lost his life in this manner was Father James Hennessey, a priest of the Boston Archdiocese, who was serving as a missioner in the Solomon Islands.

Father Hennessey was born in Cambridge, Massachusetts, September 24, 1905. He studied at St. Anselm's College, St. John's Seminary, and the North American College in Rome. He was ordained in Rome December 20, 1930, serving for a short period at Immaculate Conception, Malden, Massachusetts, and then at Boston's Cathedral parish. It was in this latter post that he met Bishop Thomas Wade, S.M., Vicar Apostolic of the North Solomon Islands, and he became convinced that at least for a time God was calling to serve as a missioner.

With the help of Father Richard Cushing, then director for the Propagation of the Faith and later Boston's Cardinal-Archbishop, permission for a mission leave was granted by Cardinal William O'Connell. Father Hennessey left for the Solomon Islands in 1936 and took up work on Bougainville Island. He was at Lemanmanu when war broke out with Japan. He had finished his five-year voluntary enlistment but agreed to stay on until a replacement was found.

On March 17, 1942, he was arrested by the Japanese and

accused of giving aid to captured Australian soldiers. He was taken first to New Ireland and kept in a native prison, where he worked in a stone quarry. In Mid-May, along with some Australian civilians, he was moved to a prisoner-of-war camp on Rabaul, where he worked on the wharves, loading and unloading ships. On June 22, 1942, he was put aboard the Japanese ship *Montevideo Maru* for transfer to a permanent prison, possibly in Japan or Hainan. About five days later, the *Montevideo Maru* was torpedoed by an American submarine off the island of Luzon in the Philippines with the loss of all life on board — 1,060 Australian prisoners of war, soldiers and civilians, including Father Hennessey and two other priests. The American submarine was not to blame, as the Japanese vessel in no way indicated it was carrying prisoners or was sailing under Red Cross protection, and thus seemed a legitimate military target.

Sources:
Ryan, George E., *Figures in Our Catholic History*
Letters, Boston Archdiocesan Archives

China

129. Father Otto A. Rauschenbach, Maryknoll (1945)

In the chaos caused by the invasion of South China by the Japanese, bandit gangs, reminiscent of the 1920s, came into being. Although some of these were Communist-inspired, other were simply unscrupulous Chinese who took advantage of a lack of government control to prey upon the people. It was one of those gangs that murdered Father Otto Rauschenbach.

Father Rauschenbach was born in St. Louis, Missouri, on June 23, 1898. He was attending the St. Louis Preparatory Seminary when he heard of the new American mission society. Attracted, he applied was accepted, and entered Maryknoll November 4, 1918. He was ordained there on June 15, 1924, and left that summer for mission work in Kongmoon, China.

Father Rauschenbach was assigned to Sancian Island, death site of St. Francis Xavier, to study Chinese with two "veteran" Maryknollers. While there, he was captured by Chan Chuk Sam, a notorious pirate, but managed to escape after a week's captivity. The following year he was transferred to Sun Chong, where he began a mission method he followed for the next two decades. He opened a medical dispensary, which he used to break down prejudice and indifference. In 1927 he was sent to Wan Fau (Closed Port), where he began from scratch, having but one Catholic. He founded a dispensary and reading room and in time had enough converts to build a substantial compound.

The story of beginning over again was repeated in other towns. In June 1935, he was assigned to open work in Dosing, beginning again with no Catholics, no money or property, but with zeal and trust in the Lord. He rented a house, opened a dispensary and reading room, and was elated when 1,500 people passed in and out on the first day. He established stations in outlying market towns and within five years was reporting to Maryknoll, "Things are beginning to break and we have all the converts we can handle in our limited accommodations."

Father Rauschenbach was visiting his outstations in May 1945, during perilous times. In recent years he'd had to flee both bandits and Japanese but had avoided confrontation. For his safety the mission superior had asked him to move to Loting, where there was better protection, and he agreed to go there after celebrating Pentecost with his converts. He spent the night of May 13 in a small market town, Kaai Lam. Leaving early the next morning, he was seized a mile out of town by bandits who pulled him off the road. Two women working on a nearby hill saw him captured.

They said that he broke away and ran, jumping down to a rice-paddy path. The robbers fired a shot, and the women heard him cry for help. They fled to give the alarm, but by the time help reached the missioner, he was dead. His pockets had been turned inside out and everything taken, including his glasses, umbrella, and the little knapsack he carried. The villagers pulled the body from a ditch, laid it on a pallet, covered it with straw, and sent word to officials.

Two Maryknoll missioners went out to reclaim the body. They found it swollen from the hot weather, the face black from a hemorrhage. A bullet had entered under the right shoulder blade and had passed through the heart. They were unable to bring the remains back to the mission center because the river and roads were controlled by the Japanese, so they had to bury him near where he had fallen.

Sources:
St. Louis Post, June 6, 1945
Maryknoll Archives

China

130. Brother Benedict Jensen, Franciscan (1947)

Following World War II, the Chinese Communists moved to take possession of the country from the ruling Kuomintang. One of their strongholds was Shantung Province in northeast China, where Franciscans from a number of nations had established missions. Franciscans from the Santa Barbara (California) Province were working in the Yaowan district.

Mission work at this time was difficult and perilous. The Reds, contemptuous of the Christian religion, were by policy tearing down churches and mission buildings. Where they exercised control, Catholic schools were closed and

Christians forbidden to pray. The people themselves were very upset as the Communists were conscripting men, women, and children into their ranks. The German Franciscan center at Tsinan was not yet in the control of the Reds, and it was crowded with refugee missioners who had been forced to flee to escape the persecution. The California Franciscan area was also relatively quiet as 1946 ended, but the priests did not know how long the calm would last.

Then, on January 1, 1947, Reds attacked the Yaowan Mission, which was staffed by Father Augustine Holzum, O.F.M., a German Franciscan from Cologne who had come south to help the Americans, and Brother Benedict Jensen, an American from Santa Barbara. The Reds caught the two missioners before they could escape, tied them up, looted the mission, and then before leaving clubbed and stabbed them to death. When the bodies were found Brother Benedict had six stab wounds, including the fatal one in his throat, and Father Augustine had been stabbed twenty times and had his skull fractured.

Brother Benedict was born John Jensen in Copenhagen, Denmark, on December 24, 1889. He emigrated early to the United States and California. At the age of thirty years, he applied to join the Franciscans at Santa Barbara as a lay brother. He was accepted and received the habit in 1920. He made his perpetual vows on October 21, 1924. He was buried in China.

Sources:
Private notes
Letter from China, Feb. 5, 1947, Franciscan Archives, St. Louis

Korea

131. Father James Maginn, Columban (1950)

When the North Korean Communists invaded South Korea in 1950, they overran a number of Catholic missions, which they looted, in some cases killing the missionaries. That these murders were done in hatred of religion is evident from the fact that, although some Americans were killed, priests of other nations were also arrested and put to death. Among the first to be killed was Father James Maginn.

Born in 1911 in Butte, Montana, he joined the Columban Fathers and was sent to the Columban headquarters in Ireland to complete his studies. He was ordained in Ireland in 1935 and the following year left for Mokpo, Korea. He was interned in a Japanese concentration camp during World War II. When peace came, he was assigned to pioneer work in the new Columban Vicariate of Chunchion, where he was put in charge of a new mission at Samchok.

Father Maginn was at Samchok when the Reds invaded the south. He had ample time to flee but deliberately chose to remain with his Christians, who he believed would need him in the dark days ahead. On July 2, 1950, the Reds reached Samchok. John Kim, the first Samchok convert of Father Maginn and an English teacher at the local high school who was living with the priest and teaching him Korean, went out after breakfast in order to buy food for the mission when he was captured by the Reds and jailed. Father Maginn sent a messenger to the prison with a note for Kim, exhorting him to keep the Faith and promising prayers.

On July 4, Communists came to the mission. They removed church equipment with the personal effects of Father Maginn and John Kim, along with all books. Father Maginn was taken to prison and put into the cell alongside that of John Kim. Over the next two days, the priest was questioned, threatened, and abused. At midnight of July 7, 1950, Father Maginn was taken from his cell, marched to a wooded section outside town, and shot. The Reds left his body where it fell. It was discovered by the mother of Father Maginn's cook, who buried it.

In the lull that came in the war after the North Koreans were driven back north by American forces and before the Chinese Communists invaded, a Columban went to Samchok seeking information on Father Maginn. He was told of the priest's murder but was unable to find the grave as the cook's mother had fled with other refugees. Through 1951 the search went on. Then shortly after 1952 began, the old woman was found in Pusan. She returned to Samchok and located the grave. The body of the slain missioner was exhumed, uncovered, and clearly identified. Father Maginn had been shot in the head. His skull was fractured, but there was no way of knowing whether this was before or after death. His left leg was also broken.

The body was taken to the mission center at Chunchon, where it was buried beneath a Celtic cross, alongside two Irish Columbans who had also been killed by the Communists.

Sources:

NCWC News Service, March 3, 1951

Burke, Patrick, unpublished summary, January 15, 1958

Kim, John, "My Last Hours with Father Maginn," September 4, 1951

Department of State, Report of Death, May 8, 1952

The Far East, June 1952

Korea

132. Monsignor Patrick T. Brennan, Columban (1950)

Among those who disappeared during the North Korean invasion of South Korea was Monsignor Patrick T. Brennan from Chicago, who was arrested along with two Irish Columbans.

Patrick T. Brennan was born in Chicago, March 13,

1901. His father was a city fireman, and for a time the son thought of following in his father's career. He attended parochial schools in Chicago and then entered St. Rita's High School for a two-year commercial course, at the end of which he went to work for a railroad company. However, after a year of commerce, he told his parents that he wished to become a priest and, with their blessing, entered Quigley Preparatory Seminary. He advanced to St. Mary of the Lake Seminary, Mundelein, Illinois, and was ordained April 14, 1928 as a Chicago diocesan priest.

Father Brennan's first assignment was to Epiphany Parish in Chicago, where he served for five years. He was transferred to St. Mary's of the Lake Parish, an assignment he hoped would be temporary. He had applied to Cardinal Mundelein for permission to join St. Columban's Foreign Mission Society in order to work in overseas missions. The cardinal told him that he would allow such an application if Father Brennan would serve in the Home Mission Band for a year, preaching parish missions during the cardinal's jubilee year. He fulfilled this assignment and then served in St. Anthony's Church in Joliet until the Columban acceptance came in 1936.

The following year, Father Brennan sailed for Korea and was stationed in Chunchon. When the Japanese opened the war with the United States at the end of 1941, he was arrested by the Japanese military, who years earlier had occupied Korea, and jailed in an internment camp. A year later, Japanese citizens caught in the United States by the war and American civilians held by Japan were exchanged and repatriated. When Father Brennan arrived home, since mission work in the Orient was at a standstill, he asked for and received permission to become a chaplain in the United States Army. He served in Europe, and at war's end, having survived the Battle of the Bulge, he was discharged with the rank of major and with battle decorations.

With peace once again in the Orient, Father Brennan returned to Korea in 1946. The following year he was named director of Columban missions in China, Burma, and Korea and took up residence in Shanghai. A man of many talents and of quick Irish wit, he was a popular choice when Rome selected him as the prefect apostolic of Mokpo, Korea, the final step before becoming a bishop. He returned to Korea in 1948, made his headquarters in Mokpo, and was there when the Red invasion took place. He sent most of his priests south to safety but remained behind with several priests to care for his Christians. In his last letter to Columban headquarters in Ireland, written July 5, 1950, he reported that the fighting was two hundred miles away, that there was no need to worry, and that he was so confident of victory that some of the priests were setting out tomato plants. He ended by saying he was "not going to be disturbed by rumors."

Twenty days later the Reds were in Mokpo and he was arrested along with two Irish priests who had remained with him. He was held in the Mokpo jail for a time and then moved to a prison in Kwangju, where some captured American GIs later reported that he had lost weight since they were only fed a bowl of rice gruel a day. One GI who survived the war and imprisonment reported that the priests were a boon to their morale: "They boosted it by at least five hundred percent!"

After almost two months of this imprisonment, the priests and soldiers were put aboard trucks, tied with ropes to prevent escape. They traveled for three nights, spending the days in local jails. Their destination was Taejon, but seven miles from the city their truck broke down, and they had to walk the rest of the way with difficulty. The soldiers were suffering from wounds, and some were barefoot. Monsignor Brennan, weakened by the ordeal and by lack of food, had to be supported by one of his priests. In Taejon the priests were separated from the soldiers, who were to be moved on to Pyongyang. Monsignor Brennan had buoyed them with the advice, "Trust in God and everything will come out all right in the end."

From the departure of the soldiers, news of the missioners is sketchy. From what can be put together, the three priests were taken to the Franciscan Monastery in Taejon, where other parishioners were held. The Catholic wife of a Korean judge, herself a prisoner, saw them there and later described them. The woman was released on September 24, 1950, as the Reds were preparing to retreat north. That night there was a massacre of all the prisoners in the monastery. The retreating Communists left behind thousands of bodies, some of which Koreans buried and others which were found by advancing American and ROK troops. A Maryknoll priest and a Parish Foreign Missioner came in behind the Americans and reported that the corpses were so swollen and decomposed that recognition was nearly impossible. Only after great difficulty were the remains of a Paris Foreign Missioner identified. The Columbans, who made a thorough investigation after the area was reclaimed, concluded that Monsignor Brennan and the two Irish priests were slain in the Taejon holocaust on September 24 and are probably interred in the mass graves there.

Sources:
The New World, Chicago, December 1, 1950
Makarounis, Alexander, *I Survived the Korean Death March*
Brennan, Patrick, Letter to Superior General, July 5, 1950
Columban U.S. Archives

133. Bishop Patrick J. Byrne, Maryknoll (1950)

Bishop Patrick J. Byrne was a pioneer of the Maryknoll Fathers' mission work in Korea, but from the time of that work and until his death there, he had a varied career.

Bishop Byrne was born in Washington, D.C., October 26, 1888. He studied for the priesthood of the Baltimore Archdiocese and was ordained at St. Mary's Seminary there on June 23, 1915. He had received permission to join the Catholic Foreign Mission Society, which had been founded three years earlier, and thus became the first priest to enter Maryknoll. Gifted with a wonderful sense of humor and intellectually talented, he served as director of the preparatory seminary in Clarks Summit, Pennsylvania, and as rector of the major seminary at Maryknoll, New York. When in 1922 Maryknoll was assigned a territory in Korea, bordering Manchuria along the Yalu River, larger than Massachusetts and Connecticut combined, Father Byrne was appointed superior to open the area.

When the Holy See assigned Maryknoll a new territory in Japan, centered around the city of Kyoto, Father Byrne was transferred there in 1935 to begin that work. The mission was made a prefecture in 1937, and Father Byrne was named prefect with the title of Monsignor. Whereas convert work in Korea had been very productive, that in Kyoto was slow and difficult; an average of four converts per priest a year was considered good. In order to make the Church better known, Monsignor Byrne opened a tuberculosis hospital, the first in an area where the disease was prevalent.

As the political situation between the United States and Japan became more complex, Father Byrne in 1940 presented his resignation to the Holy See with a recommendation that a Japanese priest be made administrator. This was done, and when war broke out at the end of the following year, the mission was Japanese-directed. While the other American priests in the Kyoto region were interned, Monsignor Byrne, because of his hospital and other charities, was allowed to spend the war years in his own house. When surrender came, Japanese authorities asked him to speak on national radio and assure the people that there would be no wholesale slaughter or unjust arrests. At war's end, in the early days of the occupation, he worked closely with General MacArthur.

More honors awaited the veteran missioner. In 1947 he was named Apostolic Visitor, or papal representative, to the new South Korean Government. Two years later the embassy was raised to the rank of Apostolic Delegation and Monsignor Byrne was named a bishop, to be consecrated in Seoul on June 14, 1949. When, on Sunday, June 25, 1950, the Communists crossed the Yalu and marched on Seoul, Bishop Byrne had no thought of leaving. He believed it to be his duty to remain in Seoul and offer what religious support he could to the Korean clergy and Christians. His secretary, fellow Maryknoller Father William Booth, volunteered to stay with him.

On Wednesday the Reds reached the capital, and armed looters stripped the delegation of anything of value. When Bishop Byrne and Father Booth were arrested, they were confined to a crowded makeshift jail where they were given a handful of rice and barley and a little water each day. With them were some elderly Paris Foreign Missioners and a Korean priest; Monsignor Quinlan, an Irish-born Columban; the superior of the Chartres Sisters, and others.

After nine days, the prisoners were moved north to Pengyang, where years earlier Bishop Byrne had begun his Korean work. The rest of his captivity was spent in his old mission. In Pengyang, conditions were even worse than in Seoul. Their daily ration was a few ounces of rice and some water. When General MacArthur began his counterattack in September, the prisoners were herded into boxcars and moved farther north. The Americans advanced, and on October 21, 1950, the prisoners, now joined by captive GIs, many wounded, were ordered to leave and make a forced march along the Yalu River. The weather had turned cold; snow was already on the mountains, and Bishop Byrne and Father Booth suffered greatly as they had been arrested in light summer clothing. On one day of the march, twenty-one captured American soldiers were shot, and when the Chartres Superior collapsed, she too was shot. When the group reached its destination, far up the Yalu, three elderly Paris Foreign Missioners died within days of one another. It was here also that Bishop Byrne caught pneumonia. About twenty prisoners were crowded into the hut with Bishop Byrne, who told them: "I consider it the greatest privilege of my life to have suffered for Christ with you."

As the bishop grew weaker, Red guards ordered that he and a Father Cobos, a Paris priest who was ill with tuberculosis, be isolated in a nearby hut. Monsignor Quinlan tried to talk the guards out of the move because the Siberian wind had made it very cold, but they were adamant. Monsignor Quinlan and Father Booth helped the two sick men to the assigned hut. It had no windows and only a straw mat served as a door to keep out the wind. The sick men were put down on some straw on the floor. For four days Bishop Byrne lay in this freezing poverty. Because he was failing rapidly, Father Cobos gave him absolution, and the next day, November 25, 1950, Bishop Byrne died.

Monsignor Quinlan, Father Booth, and two others were given permission to bury the bishop. Monsignor Quinlan dressed the shriveled, emaciated body in his own cassock. They hacked a shallow grave in the frozen ground and laid the dead bishop to rest. They covered the grave with stones, a fortunate decision because crows and animals ate the bodies of others who died over that terrible winter. For three more years Monsignor Quinlan and Father Booth were held prisoners, and after the armistice they were sent home through Soviet Russia to tell the story of the last days of the bishop-martyr, whose mission career had made a full circle, beginning and ending in North Korea.

Sources:
Nevins, Albert J., *The Meaning of Maryknoll*
Maryknoll Archives

134. Bishop Francis Xavier Ford, Maryknoll (1952)

When Francis X. Ford went to China as a young priest, he wrote a prayer which became an invocation for his life: "Grant us, Lord, to be the doorstep by which the multitudes may come to worship Thee. And if, in the saving of their souls, we are ground underfoot and spat upon and worn out, at least we shall have served Thee in some small way in helping pagan souls and we shall have become the King's Highway in pathless China." The prayer was also a prophecy of his life and death.

The story of Bishop Ford began in Brooklyn on January 11, 1892, the day he was born to Elizabeth and Austin Ford, the crusading publisher of *The Irish World*. The child was baptized in Sacred Heart Church and given the name of the great apostle to the East, Francis Xavier. While his father may have hoped that his son would join him in journalism, young Francis wanted solely to be a priest and went for his formative years to the New York preparatory seminary, Cathedral College in Manhattan. It was there he met Father James A. Walsh, the co-founder of Maryknoll, and in 1912 he was accepted as the first seminarian of the new society, attending St. Joseph's Seminary in Yonkers, New York, for his advanced studies. He was ordained December 5, 1917, and left for China on September 7, 1918, as a member of the first Maryknoll departure group.

The early Maryknoll Missioners worked under the supervision of the Paris Foreign Missioners. After they had proved themselves, they were assigned the territory of Kongmoon, where Bishop James Edward Walsh, a classmate of Ford and himself a Communist prisoner for many years, was the first bishop. In 1925, the Paris society offered Maryknoll another territory in the northeast corner of Kwangtung Province, inhabited by Hakka-speaking people.

Bishop Francis Xavier Ford, M.M., martyred in China, 1947

Father Ford was put in charge, picking Kaying, the Hakka cultural center, as his own main base, and set about developing the area. His first act was to begin a seminary, giving his reason as, "A country without a native clergy is always in danger of being stranded for lack of a pilot. In time of persecution, the first to be wiped out or driven out is the foreigner." He also founded a native community of Sisters.

In 1929 the area was made into a prefecture apostolic, with Father Ford named its first prefect. All was not peaceful, however. Communists were active in his area, and mission reports tell of Christian refugees, seminarians being sent home for fear of being cut off, postponed retreats, a German Dominican killed by the Reds in an adjoining province, and so on. One of Monsignor Ford's own priests, Father Harry Bush, was held for two months by Reds until pursuing government troops brought freedom. Yet despite the troubles, the mission grew: a Catholic paper, 18 schools, a new seminary, a novitiate for Sisters, three student hostels, and 18 centers with 385 outstations.

The Holy See was pleased with the progress and in 1935 raised the mission to a vicariate and named Monsignor Ford its first bishop. He was ordained bishop at Maryknoll on September 5. He chose as his episcopal motto the Latin word *Condolere* — "To suffer with." He wished to be identified with the Chinese people. He had given his life to their service and never wanted to withdraw any of the gift. When World War II came, he established a major seminary because he could no longer send his seminarians out. He set up relief operations to care for the refugees who crowded the area, encouraging his missioners to establish rice banks, cooperatives and other social-action projects. In his last report to Maryknoll in 1950, he gave a detailed picture of an active and well-developed mission. Kaying then had two-score Chinese priests and he predicted he would be succeeded by a Chinese whom he had trained.

Then the Reds came to Hakkaland and began to draw

the noose tight, turning Kaying into a prison. Bishop Ford was arrested, his priests put on trial and exiled, his Chinese priests jailed, his Chinese Sisters sent home with instructions to marry, his seminary closed. Bishop Ford's own arrest came two days before Christmas 1950. Red soldiers entered the mission and confined the bishop to his room while they ransacked the house, taking all the mission files. An interrogator was brought from Peking to gather "evidence," and long periods of questioning followed. A note Bishop Ford smuggled out to one of his priests said: "They kept at me for five hours steady today, and I am exhausted. Mostly questions about money to support the native priests. . . . They have nothing serious on me, and I refuse to worry."

But the Communists could fabricate charges, and they filled the papers with them, printing them even in *Pravda* in Moscow. He was accused of being the head of a United States spy ring, saboteur of the Communist national-church movement, harborer of agents of the Kuomintang, organizer of an army to overthrow the People's Government — big lies, but made believable by constant repetition.

On the morning of April 14, 1951, Bishop Ford and a Maryknoll Sister who served as the mission secretary, Sister Joan Marie, were dragged bound from the mission and paraded through the main streets of Kaying. Both were bound like common criminals, the bishop's hands tied behind his back, with another rope around his neck and looped around his hands, so that when he tried to lower his hands, he pulled his head back. Red cheerleaders went along the streets, stirring up the people to shout condemnatory slogans.

They were moved to Hingning, another mission town. Bishop and Sister were forced to pass through a gauntlet of shouting and screaming students, armed with sticks, stones, and garbage. As the missioners moved along, the crowd rained blows down, stones struck with thickening thuds, and garbage and refuse covered the victims. Bishop

Ford was spit upon, tripped up, and kicked. Because of the way he was tied, he had no way to defend himself. In jail that night, people were marched past their cells to heap abuse on the American spies. In the beginning, it was the Red technique to give a political cast to their arrests of missioners so that they could not be accused of "anti-religion." The ordeal went to other towns: Laulung, Ho-yun, Waichow, Chengmatau, where a rope was run out from under the bishop's cassock so that it looked like a monkey's tail, which caused laughter and jeers for the humiliated American.

Finally, the federal prison in Canton was reached and the prisoners separated — Bishop Ford to the men's section, Sister Joan Marie to the women's. Sister Joan Marie, who was eventually released, told what happened to her, and it can be presumed that the same if not more was given to Bishop Ford. She was placed in a small, narrow cell that reminded her of the bottom of an elevator shaft. The seventeen prisoners there had to sleep on the floor and exist on meager rations. No blankets were furnished, nor soap, nor washbasin. For two months the prisoner underwent daily and seemingly endless interrogation and brainwashing — sessions that were marked by threats of violence, screams, and denunciations.

When Sister was finally removed to the main section of the prison, conditions were a little better. The cells were still crowded and dirty, the food poor, but the brainwashing was over and only interrogation remained. Sister Joan Marie was assigned the job of water carrier, which gave her limited movement about the prison. In July she got a brief sight of the bishop. He seemed tired but otherwise in good health. The year 1951 passed into 1952. One day early in January, Sister Joan Marie, going about her work, slipped on the wet floor. Prone, she looked through a door, slatted for ventilation. She saw a prisoner laboriously descending stairs, and over his shoulders, like a sack of potatoes, he was carrying another prisoner — Bishop Ford. When they reached the floor, the prisoner set the bishop down on his feet. His hair had turned white, and his Chinese gown hung loosely on his frame. The bishop tried to walk with a cane but collapsed. The man helped him to his feet and carried him off down a corridor. In February, Sister Joan Marie again saw the bishop being carried, but her own malnutrition had left her weak so that she only noted the main incident, not details.

On August 16, Sister Joan Marie was taken to the warden's office, where she was told that Bishop Ford was dead. She was ordered to sign a statement that Bishop Ford had died from illness and old age. Knowing the death had resulted from ill-treatment, she tried to resist, but in her weakened condition she yielded to the Communists' persuasion and signed. In doing so, she noted the date of death, February 21, 1952, a few days after she had last seen him. The Communists then moved her to the prison hospital, not wanting her to die in their hands. On September 2, she was told that in a few days the "crimes" of Bishop Ford would be released to the public, and the people's reaction would be hard to control, so to protect her life they were deporting her at once. Two soldiers took her to the Hong Kong border, where she crossed the bridge to freedom and revealed to the world the persecution Bishop Ford endured.

Sources:
Nevins, Albert J., *The Meaning of Maryknoll*
Lane, Raymond A., *Stone in the King's Highway*
Maryknoll Archives

Bolivia

135. Father William Carl Kruegler, Maryknoll (1962)

Father William Carl Kruegler was born in Troy, New York, on October 1, 1930, attending Sacred Heart School

144

and Catholic Central High School there. After graduating from high school, he entered Maryknoll College, Lakewood, New Jersey, to prepare for the foreign mission priesthood. He was ordained at Maryknoll Seminary, Maryknoll, New York, on June 8, 1957. Shortly after ordination, he left for his mission assignment in Bolivia, serving in parishes in Cochabamba, Cotoca, and finally Montero.

In Montero he was stationed at Our Lady of Mercy Parish, where he was very popular with the people, particularly the young. One of the problems in Montero was a saloon that adjoined the church. It was a place of much noise and rowdyism. Father Krueglar was particularly disturbed that the bar owner allowed children to patronize the place. The priest had made a number of protests to the saloon keeper without any result.

On Tuesday morning, August 7, 1962, at six o'clock, Father Kruegler went to the bar again to complain that the noise was interfering with Mass. The bar owner, Manglio Saravia, appeared at the door naked and ridiculed the priest. Later that morning Father Kruegler went to the police and filed a complaint that the bar was serving liquor without a license and that children were allowed to congregate there. The police then warned Saravia.

As evening approached, Saravia showed up several times around the rectory asking for Father Kruegler, only to be told that he was out. About seven P.M. as the priest was entering the rectory, Savaria stepped from the shadows and seemed to ask a question of the priest. As Father Kruegler turned, the bar owner fired a pistol at point-blank range. The priest slumped to the ground, and the enraged man fired four more times. He had missed twice, but three of the bullets found their marks, hitting the priest in the neck, shoulder and chest. Hearing the shots, other priests rushed from the rectory. One gave Father Kruegler the last rites while another rushed him to the hospital, but he was dead on arrival.

News of the shooting brought a crowd to the mission, and as people became more and more incensed, the pastor of the parish sought to calm them. However, when word of Father Kruegler's death came from the hospital, the crowd became an uncontrollable mob, which then stormed the saloon. Savaria was found and dragged across the street to the town plaza, where he was hanged from a tree.

The slain priest was waked in the parish church, where the rosary was said constantly. Thousands of people turned out for the funeral, and the church could only hold a small proportion of them. Father Kruegler was buried in the garden of the church, so that he could remain with the people he had adopted. Years earlier when he was a youth, his sister, who was to become a Maryknoll Sister, had asked him, "What is a martyr?" He had replied, "It's when someone comes up to you with a gun and says, 'Do you believe in God?' and if you say 'yes,' he shoots you. That's a martyr."

Sources:
The Evangelist (Albany, New York), October 16, 1986
The New York Times, August 9, 1962
Maryknoll Archives

Wisconsin

136. Father Marcellus Cabo, Franciscan (1974)

Writing in a Franciscan publication, *Lesser Brothers*, the distinguished Franciscan historian Father Marion Habig said, "Father Marcellus died a real martyr of the Faith." Father Habig identified the priest with the Franciscan martyrs of the Great Pueblo Revolt of 1680, killed at the behest of medicine men who rejected Christian culture.

Father Marcellus Cabo was born of Croatian ancestry in Chicago, Illinois, on June 2, 1915, receiving the name

Martin at baptism. He attended Chicago schools and entered the Franciscan Sacred Heart Province on August 19, 1935. He was ordained a priest on June 24, 1942. After one year in a parish at Ashland, he was, because of his ancestry, loaned to the Croatian Franciscan Commissariat in the United States and served in various parishes until 1952, when he returned to his province.

That same year he was assigned to St. Anthony Parish, Neopit, Wisconsin, where he was to remain until his death. The parish was largely composed of Menominee Indians, whom Father Marcellus came to love and who loved him in return. Over the years he completed building a church, school, convent, and rectory. He encouraged the Indians in their native crafts and opened a gift shop where they could sell their handcrafted garments and other art. He did this not only to preserve ancient traditions, but also to provide income for needy Indians. He also encouraged the Indians to improve their homes, on one occasion going to Chicago to beg paint that they could use.

In the late sixties, a native movement began to spread among the Indians, called the American Indian Movement. While the Indians in various parts of the United States had many legitimate grievances, some elements of this movement rejected anything white, including religion. In some areas there was violence and confrontation, often spurred by white activists, which on more than one occasion resulted in deaths of both Indians and whites.

Some dissidents among the Menominees formed a movement called the "Menominee Warriors Society," which sought to exploit Indian grievances. Among targets of the Warriors' hatred was the Catholic Church. It was this group that was to seize the Alexian Brothers notiviate at Gresham, Wis., and hold it over a month. Menominee leaders disapproved of the group, saying its members were not representative of the tribe and were "known more for their consumption of alcohol and drugs than for their civic-mindedness." John LaTengar, a member of this group, on Thanksgiving Day, November 28, 1974, broke into the Neopit rectory at two A.M. and brutally murdered Father Marcellus, inflicting eight stab wounds, two in the heart area, and a cut across the throat. Later, after the Indian was apprehended by police, he said he only wanted to rob the rectory. However, those close to the situation said that Warrior teachings were the cause. Father William Spalding, of the nearby parish at Shawano, declared that Father Marcellus "was murdered because of a prevailing deep hatred for the Catholic Church and Christianity." Menominee leaders deplored the death and extolled the priest, one stating, "Ever since Father has been here, he has put his heart and soul into helping the Indian people."

Funeral services for the slain priest were held at his church, attended by three bishops, twenty priests, and five hundred mourners. The body was taken for burial to the Franciscan Cemetery in Oak Brook, Illinois.

Sources:
Appleton (Wisconsin) *Post-Crescent*, December 1, 1974
Green Bay (Wisconsin) *Press Gazette*, November 29, 1975
National Catholic Reporter, Vol. 11, No. 17
Habig, Marion, unpublished notes

Honduras

137. Father Casimir Cypher, Conventual Franciscan (1975)

Father Casimir Cypher, O.F.M. Conv., was born on June 9, 1939, into a Medford, Wisconsin, farming family that consisted of nine boys and three girls. He was baptized Michael in his parish church. At the age of eighteen he entered the Conventual Novitiate of St. Bonaventure in Lake

Father Casimir Cypher, O.F.M. Conv., martyred in Honduras, 1975

Forest, Illinois, to prepare for the Franciscan priesthood, and it was here that he was given the religious name of Casimir. He finished his studies at Loyola University in Chicago and was ordained in 1968.

Father Casimir's first assignment was to St. Anthony's Church in Rockford. It was here that his desire to be a missioner came into flower, and he volunteered for work in a Franciscan mission in Honduras. In 1972 his superiors sent him to the Spanish-speaking Parish of Our Lady of Guadalupe in Hermosa Beach, California, where he would have the opportunity to learn some Spanish. Finally, 1974 found Father Casimir as assistant pastor at St. Jerome's Parish in Gualaco, Honduras.

The young priest, although not yet proficient in Spanish, spoke a language of love. The people, especially children, were attracted to him, and no sacrifice was too much for him to make for them. The parish covered about five hundred square miles and Father Casimir was frequently in the saddle, covering outlying districts. An American lay missioner who worked with him described him as a "stocky thirty-five-old priest, who had a sincere love for and felt at ease with the poor, the elderly and the sick. When first you met him you thought what a simple man this was. Then you came to understand his intelligence, his deep spirituality, the way he loved all things, the way he wanted most of all to serve God and to help the people, and you understood that this was a most unusual man."

On one trip into the back country, Father Casimir was bitten on the hand by an insect. The bite resulted in an infection that left him with a high fever and great weakness. Because of the lack of medical facilities in his mountainous post, his superiors sent him in October 1974 to the United States for treatment. Cured, he was back in Honduras shortly after the first of the new year.

This time he was sent alone to the village of San Esteban to begin a new mission among people who had long been praying that a priest would come and live among them. He quickly won the farmers by his simple ways, and he was able to get around the rutted roads of his parish more easily because Catholic Relief Services had furnished him with a truck. The vehicle also enabled him to move sick people to the hospital and was the means of saving lives. It was such a trip that cost him his own life.

On June 25, 1975, Father Casimir took an injured peasant into the provincial capital of Juticalpa for treatment. While there, he decided to have some repairs made to the truck and, while waiting for the work to be finished, walked into the center of town. Unknown to him, peasants of the area were gathering to demand the land reform the government had promised. The movement was led by the Farmers National Union, which had the support of the bishop of the diocese; he had set up a *campesino* training center in the diocese in which some priests, nuns, and lay missioners were active. This in turn infuriated the wealthy landowners, who were in league with military units, labeling the diocese's efforts at justice as "Communism."

It was into this situation that Father Casimir walked. He was stopped by soldiers who were arresting land-reform leaders and seeking a French priest, Father Michael Piton, who had been counseling peasants. Unknown to Father Casmir, there had also been some shooting violence earlier that day. The soldiers asked him for identification, and he showed them his American driving license which was issued in his legal name of Michael. Although he protested that he was Father Casimir from San Esteban and that he was not an activist, he was led off by the soldiers, who refused to believe the coincidence. He was taken to the jail where he was beaten to make him "confess." That night he was taken, along with some others who had been arrested, to a ranch outside town where he was shot along with the others. Their bodies were thrown into a deep well, and a sergeant tossed in several sticks of dynamite to try and close it from search.

El Salvador Martyrs, 1980 (from left): above, Sister Maura Clarke, M.M.; Sister Ita Ford, M.M.; below, Sister Dorothy Kazel, O.S.U., and Jean Donovan, lay missioner

It was not until mid-July that pressure from the Church caused the government to follow up leads to the murders. The well was opened and the bodies brought up. Besides Father Casimir and several peasants, the remains included: Father Ivan Betancourt, a Colombian priest: Mary Elena Bolivar, a lay missioner from Colombia; and Ruth García, a student leader. Father Casmir's body was taken to his former Gualaco parish for burial. People from all over the province streamed in for the funeral. After the funeral Mass and testimonies by students who knew him, the remains were laid to rest in the mission church. He was the first American to be killed by reactionary groups in Central America.

Sources:
Immaculata, September, 1975
Chicago Tribune, July 20, 1975
Our Sunday Visitor, August 31, 1975
Maryknoll Magazine, September, 1982

El Salvador

138. Sister Maura Clarke, Maryknoll (1980)
139. Sister Ita Ford, Maryknoll
140. Sister Dorothy Kazel, Ursuline
141. Jean Donovan, Lay Missioner

For almost 430 years, from 1542 when Father Juan Padilla died in Kansas until 1980, there were no women Religious martyrs connected with the United States. Then in 1980 there were three of them: Sister Maura Clarke, M.M., Sister Ita Ford, M.M., and Sister Dorothy Kazel, O.S.U., plus Jean Donovan, a lay missioner. These women fell victim to Salvadoran oligarchs who considered the Church's apostolic work in behalf of the poor as subversive.

At the time of their murders, El Salvador was held in the terror of rightist death squads, composed of military and civilians, that had brought death to nine thousand Salvadorans. Among these victims was Archbishop Oscar Romero of San Salvador, who in a sermon declared: "Martyrdom is a grace of God that I do not feel worthy of. But if God accepts the sacrifice of my life, my hope is that my blood will be like a seed of liberty and a sign that our aspirations will soon become a reality." Although the bloodbath unleashed by those who opposed the Church's Gospel-based justice had brought death to many priests and other Church workers, no nun had been killed until the four Americans were slain.

Sister Maura Clarke (baptized Mary) was born in the Bronx, New York, on January 13, 1931. As a child she moved with her family to the Brooklyn Diocese, where she attended St. Francis de Sales School in Rockaway and Stella Maris High School. She entered the Maryknoll Sisters in 1950, and after training she was assigned to a Maryknoll convent in the Bronx. In 1959 she went to Nicaragua and was sent to Siuna, a gold-mining town in the mountains, where she taught school and did social work. In 1969 she was transferred to the capital, Managua, where she helped form basic Christian communities and trained leaders for catechetical work.

Sister Maura was in Managua when a massive earthquake leveled most of the city. She helped dig the trapped out of ruins and cared for the injured. She returned to the United States for some continuing education, and then in 1980 she was sent to El Salvador to work with Sister Ita Ford, who had lost her companion-Sister to drowning in a flooded river. Not long before her death she wrote home: "What is happening here is impossible, but happening. The endurance of the poor and their faith through this terrible pain is constantly pulling me to a deeper faith response. My fear of death is being challenged constantly as children, lovely young girls, and old people are being shot and some cut up with machetes and bodies thrown by the road, and people prohibited from burying them."

Sister Ita Catherine Ford was born in Brooklyn, April 23, 1940. She was the grandniece of Bishop Francis X. Ford, himself a martyr in China. She attended Fontbonne Hall in Brooklyn and graduated from Marymount College. She worked for some years as an editor for a publisher of religious and school textbooks and in 1971 entered Maryknoll, where she was known for her outgoing personality and sense of humor. Her first mission assignment was in 1972 to Chile, where for the first time she experienced the suffering of people in poverty. She worked to form basic Christian communities and identify herself with the people. She wrote home to say that she had no solutions for the suffering of the powerless and that all she could do was to walk with the people.

Sister Ita was reassigned to El Salvador in the spring of 1980, shortly after the murder of Archbishop Romero. She was amazed to find that in El Salvador feeding the hungry could be considered a subversive act. With Sister Carol Piette, she worked on an emergency refugee committee in Chalatenango. It was there she almost drowned in a flash flood that took the life of Sister Carol. She wondered why God had allowed her to live but had taken her companion. Because she was alone, Sister Maura was sent to work with her.

Sister Dorothy Kazel, O.S.U., was born in Cleveland, Ohio, June 30, 1939. She attended schools there and after graduation worked as a sales clerk, and medical secretary, teaching elementary school for a year. She spent one summer working at the Papago Indian Reservation in Arizona. She entered the Ursuline Community in 1960 and made her profession of religious vows on August 13, 1963. She taught for seven years at the Ursulines' Sacred Heart Academy and for two years at Beaumont School for Girls. During this time she was also quite active in community service programs, encouraging her students to aid the handicapped, elderly, and ill.

Her work with Western Indians had given Sister a taste for missionary life, plus a desire to devote herself to the poor. She found her answer in her own diocese. Cleveland, as had some other dioceses, responded to the Holy See's call for mission involvement by taking responsibility for a mission in El Salvador, staffing it with diocesan priests and lay personnel. Sister Dorothy was given permission to join this team and went to El Salvador to work in Chirilagua. The following year she was transferred to the Cleveland parish in La Unión, but two years later, when this parish was turned over to local clergy, she was moved to a parish in the port of La Libertad, where she was working at the time of her death. She was aware of the danger in which she lived, and she wrote to a Sister back home that as long as there was work to do she "wouldn't want to run out on the people." In her last letter to Cleveland friends, she spoke of El Salvador "writhing in pain" and "yearning for peace" and of the need "to continue preaching the word of the Lord even though it may mean 'laying down your life' for your fellowman."

Jean Donovan was born in Stamford, Connecticut, April 10, 1955. She grew up in a family that could give her many luxuries. She was adept at golf and horseback riding and was able to travel. Graduating from high school in Westport, Connecticut, she went to Mary Washington College in Virginia, then to University College, Cork, Ireland, and finally to Case Western Reserve University, Cleveland, graduating with degrees in political economy and management accounting. She went to work for a management consulting firm in Cleveland and was soon making a good salary.

A boisterous, fun-loving person who was the life of any party, Jean Donovan also had a serious side. She joined a young-adult ministry program sponsored by the diocese. On the questionnaire she filled out for this program she wrote: "I'd like to work with people, lonely people, who don't realize that God loves them." It was through this program that she learned of the Cleveland mission team in El Salvador. She had previously thought of joining the Peace Corps, but the Cleveland effort had greater appeal. She said, "It's every Christian's job to spread the good news that God loves us." Thus in August 1979 she joined the Cleveland team and was working in La Libertad, where she soon became a familiar figure speeding about on her motorbike. "She was our live wire," remembered Sister Martha Owen, a co-worker.

Thus the stage was set for the tragedy of December 2, 1980. Sisters Maura and Ita had gone to Nicaragua for a regional meeting of Maryknoll Sisters that evaluated the work being done and formed plans for the future. Before leaving El Salvador, they had arranged with Sister Dorothy to pick them up at the San Salvador airport on their return on December 2. The flight from Managua was delayed an hour, and at the airport that night a Canadian priest, working in El Salvador, saw Sister Dorothy and Jean Donovan. They told him they were awaiting the delayed Maryknollers. He was the last friend to see them alive.

About mid-morning the next day, Father Paul Schindler, a Cleveland priest, called the American Embassy and reported that two of his team members had gone to the airport the previous evening to pick up two sisters and had not returned home. The embassy then notified the Salvadoran police chief, who promised to put out an all-points bulletin, but there is evidence that this was never done and the embassy later called the government effort "an astonishing lack of cooperation." In any event, that day the burnt-out wreck of the minibus that the Cleveland workers used was found near the airport, and there was a growing fear that the four were dead. The next day (December 4) several peasants from Zacatecoluca, a town twenty-five miles southeast of San Salvador, went to their local priest and told him that soldiers had forced them to bury the bodies of four women in a shallow common grave on a farm outside town. The priest in turn called the Salvadoran Episcopal Conference, and Archbishop Rivera y Damas reported the information to the embassy. Ambassador Robert White personally led a team to the site, and the grave was unearthed, revealing the bodies of the four missioners. They had all been killed by bullets in their heads and there was evidence that there had been rape before the burial.

The two Maryknoll Sisters were interred at Chalatenango, where they worked, as is customary with their society. Archbishop Rivera y Damas, who came to the remote peasant village for the funeral, told the people, "We are oppressed but not defeated." Sister Dorothy Kazel's remains were flown to Cleveland, where Bishop Anthony J. Pilla, head of the diocese, spoke at the memorial service of the dangers modern missioners face for the sake of the Gospel. Sister was interred with other Ursulines. Jean Donovan's body was taken to Sarasota, Florida, where her parents were living. Bishop Thomas Larkin celebrated the funeral Mass, praising her sacrifice.

In an effort to bring the murderers to justice, the United States suspended all aid to El Salvador until progress was made in solving the killings. This and other diplomatic pressures finally caused the government to act. Some soldiers were arrested and tried after many delays. However, observers noted that those who gave the order and those who blocked the investigation were never identified.

Sources:

Maryknoll Magazine, March 1951
Our Sunday Visitor, December 21, 1980
National Catholic Reporter, December 19, 26, 1981
The New York Times, December 6, 7, 1980

Catholic Universe Bulletin (Cleveland), December 12, 19, 1980
Press releases, Ursuline and Maryknoll Sisters

Guatemala

142. Father Stanley Rother (1981)

Another victim of Central American paramilitary forces that harassed both the Church and the Indians they served was Father Stanley Rother, a priest from the Oklahoma City Archdiocese, which took responsibility for a Guatamalan parish in 1964. Father Rother was assigned to that parish, Santiago Atitlán, in 1968.

Father Rother was born on March 27, 1935, in the German farm community of Okarche, Oklahoma. He attended Holy Trinity School there, and in high school he specialized in vocational agriculture and served as president of the Future Farmers of America chapter. However, his intention of becoming a family farmer changed to a conviction that he should serve the Church as a priest, so after high school he went to Assumption Seminary in San Antonio, Texas, and then to Mount St. Mary's Seminary in Emmitsburg, Maryland. He was ordained May 25, 1963, and spent the next five years in archdiocesan parish assignments. He volunteered for work at the archdiocesan mission in Guatemala, was accepted, and left for Guatemala in 1968.

The Oklahoma City Archdiocese had responded in 1964 to Pope John XIII's appeal for First World help for the Third World. The archdiocese took responsibility for a mission on Lake Atitlán among the Tzutihil Indians, who scratched out a living from corn corps planted on steep mountainsides. The Oklahoma priests established a clinic, a Montessori school, a radio station, an experimental farm, and other projects. In the beginning there were many volunteers and at the height twelve missioners, but they left one

Father Stanley Rother, secular priest martyred in Guatemala, 1981

by one, until, after 1973, only Father Rother remained.

Father Rother, who had had difficulty with his seminary studies, became proficient in Spanish and the Tzutihil dialect. He translated the Mass prayers and readings, and he was translating the entire New Testament when he was killed. He taught the people hygiene, aided them with their crops, and encouraged the women to form cooperatives for their weaving, for which he was helping them to market their work. Always good with his hands, he renovated mission buildings and was not afraid of hard manual labor. He was respected by the people, held their affection, and brought them to the sacraments. He used fiestas to celebrate mass baptisms and marriages. Just three days before his death at the parish fiesta of St. James (Santiago) he witnessed almost a hundred marriages.

Then the troubles began. The Guatemalan Indians, long exploited and impoverished (two percent of Guatemala's 7.2 million people own 70 percent of the arable land) and making up 80 percent of the nation's population, began asking the government for justice. In some areas guerrilla activity began. The reaction of the military government and wealthy landowners was immediate repression. Through it all, Father Rother tried to remain nonpolitical, and he was critical of priests who were activists. But when the mission radio station was pillaged and the director of his radio school, Gaspar Culan, killed; when his catechist and deacon, Diego Quic, was murdered; and when his agricultural and health programs were challenged, he felt he had to protest.

In his 1980 Christmas letter home he told of the presence of soldiers in the area seeking Communist guerrillas, and added, "But there aren't any around here." He reported on ten men of the parish who were kidnapped and presumed dead. He concluded: "A nice compliment was given to me recently when a supposed leader in the church and town was complaining, 'Father is defending the people.' He wants me deported for my sin. This is one of the reasons I have for staying in the face of physical harm. The shepherd cannot run at the first sign of danger."

However, in January of 1981 he was warned that his name was on a death list. He went back to Oklahoma City to see the bishop and let things cool down. But he felt he was betraying his people. He told a close priest friend in the United States that he had to get back, saying, "I just can't abandon those good people." He said he knew he was marked for death but he was going to meet the threat "in my own way. If they ever come for me in the rectory or the church, they will have to kill me there. I will not be taken away." He told his friend how Guatemalan priests were kidnapped, tortured for days, mutilated, and then killed, with their bodies left beside a road as a warning.

In April, despite the danger, he was back in his mission to celebrate Holy Week with his flock. He had resolved to be with his people no matter what happened. The paramilitary came for Father Rother at one o'clock on the morning of July 28. They burst into his room while he was in bed, shot him through the cheek, in the head, and behind the left ear. The Indians wanted to bury Father Rother in their church, but learning that his family wanted the body back in Oklahoma, they asked for his heart. During embalming, that organ was removed and was buried in front of the altar at Santiago Atitlán. The rest of the remains were shipped to Oklahoma City, where funeral services were held in the crowded cathedral. The coffin was then taken to Okarche, where he was interred among his deceased relatives and farming friends. The murder, like all the others, went unpunished and unsolved.

Sources:
Maryknoll Magazine, January 1982
National Catholic Reporter, August 14, 1981
The Pilot (Boston), August 7, 1981
Our Sunday Visitor, October 18, 1981

Guatemala

143. Brother James Miller, Christian Brother (1982)

On a Saturday afternoon in Huehuetenango, Guatemala, Brother James Alfred Miller was making repairs on the mission school, Colegio La Salle, where he taught, when a car with four hooded men drew abreast and the occupants opened fire on him. Bullets entered his neck and chest, and he fell to the ground, dying instantaneously. The date was February 13, 1982, and he was one more victim of the undeclared war the Guatemalan right was waging against those who helped the Indians.

Huehuetenango is a small city, surrounded by Indian villages, at the foot of the Cuchumatanes Mountains. In 1942 it became the center for a modern mission effort, pioneered by the Maryknoll Fathers from the United States. In time, the American missioners developed the area to the point where it now has a Guatemalan bishop, aided by Guatemalan priests as well as foreign missioners. The Indian people subsist in a corn econony and live in great poverty. The missioners tried to raise their standard of living by developing new crops, training leaders, and beginning cooperatives. As progress was made, landowners became resentful, and in recent years, in alliance with the military, raids have been made on Indian villages with the result that thousands of Indians from the Huehuetenango, Quiche, and Peten areas have had to flee to refugee camps in Mexico to avoid slaughter.

It was in this atmosphere of hatred and militancy that Brother Miller worked. It is believed that he was not particularly singled out for any reason, but that his presence on the street outside the school made him available to his murderers, who wanted to give a warning to the Church that it should desist in aiding the Indians. The school was probably picked because several days earlier several Indian students had been seized by soldiers as "protesters" and the Brothers had made strong objections to the arrests. The school was also disliked by the wealthy because it was training native leaders who would object to the discrimination practiced all over Guatemala.

Brother Miller was born on September 22, 1944, in Ellis, Wisconsin, where his parents operated a dairy farm. He went to local schools and after a year at the local high school joined the Winona (Minnesota) province of the Christian Brothers. He was sent to the Brothers' high school in Stevens Point and after graduation there matriculated at St. Mary's College in Winona. He spent one summer vacation while at the Winona school working in Nicaragua, and he let his superiors know that he would prefer missions to be his life work.

After several assignments in the United States, he was sent to Nicaragua in 1971 and in the following nine years worked as a teacher, builder, and administrator in Bluefields with the American Capuchins and in Waspam and Puerto Cabezas. In 1980 he returned to the United States on a sabbatical and spent the year as a teacher in Cretin High School, St. Paul, Minnesota. He was reassigned to Guatemala and went there early in 1981. He taught English and religion and served as a student guidance counselor at Colegio La Salle in Huehuetenango, but he also helped run an experimental farm and the La Salle Indian House, where he supervised the care and education of 150 young highland Indians who were training as teachers. It could have been this last responsibility that cost him his life. At any event, he and the other Brothers in Huehuetenango knew the danger they were in because of their work with the Indians, having discussed it many times and agreeing that they would not allow themselves to be forced out.

164

Brother James Miller, F.S.C., martyred in Guatemala, 1982

Bishop Hugo Martínez of Huehuetenango celebrated a Mass of Resurrection the day after the death, and thousands of people walked behind the coffin the four miles to the airport. In Guatemala City more services were held, and then the coffin went to Wisconsin, where a wake was held in Stevens Point, with the final funeral Mass and burial behind St. Martin's Church in Ellis. In the final eulogy, Bishop Frederick Freking of La Crosse told the congregation, "We need to take a stand on the rights, especially of the poor. Thank God there are people like Brother James to do that."

Sources:
Statement, Guatemala Regional Superior, February 16, 1982
NC News Service, February 15, 1982
National Catholic Reporter (Edmonds article), February 28, 1982
The Tablet, Brooklyn, New York, February 20, 1982

Wisconsin

144. Father John Rossiter (1985)
145. Ferdinand Roth, Lay Minister
146. William Hammes, Layman

Changes in the Church brought about by Vatican Council II, and disapproved of by a man of questionable mental balance, resulted in a great tragedy in St. Patrick's Parish, Onalaska, Wisconsin. The event brought death to the pastor, Father John Rossiter; a lay minister, Ferdinand Roth, Sr.; and the parish custodian, William Hammes.

Father Rossiter was born in 1921 in La Crosse, Wisconsin. He was ordained in 1953 at the late age of thirty-two. He had come late to the priesthood because of military service in the South Pacific. After ordination he was assigned to teach at Regis High School in Eau Claire and was also appointed to serve as an assistant pastor at St. Patrick's Parish there. He later became principal of the high school and pastor of Holy Guardian Angels Parish in Brackett. He served as chaplain for the Wisconsin Catholic War Veterans and the American Legion. In 1968 he was named pastor of St. Patrick Parish, Onalaska, one of the larger parishes of the La Crosse Diocese. He was very popular with his people and particularly held the affection of the schoolchildren. Visiting every classroom in the parish school each week to teach religion, he was a man of warmth and ready wit. Father Rossiter was a progressive priest, implementing the changes brought about by the Council and drawing his people into the life of the Church, but was in no way radical.

Ferdinand Roth, Sr., who was fifty-five years old when he died, had retired from a thirty-three-year career with the Burlington Northern Railroad. With time to himself, Roth became interested in service to the Church. He graduated from a two-year training program for lay ministers, conducted by the diocesan office of ministries. At St. Patrick's his service was largely liturgical. He trained the parish Mass servers, brought Communion to a nursing home, and held Scripture/Rosary devotions there. He also aided with a hospice program in La Crosse. He coached a Little League team and was active with a conservation program. He was married and was survived by a wife and six children.

William Hammes was born August 16, 1918, on a farm in eastern La Cross County. He farmed in his early years and then went into the military, serving in the South Pacific Theater, where he received a Purple Heart. After the war was over, he became a trucker. When he married, he and his wife moved to a house two doors from St. Patrick's. Whenever the parish needed some repairs to be made, he volunteered his services. In 1980 he was offered the position of parish custodian, which he accepted. In his free time, he liked to hunt and fish and was a hobbyist beekeeper. He was survived by a wife and daughter.

The Onalaska tragedy took place following an eight

Father John Rossiter, secular priest martyred in Wisconsin, 1985

o'clock Mass on the morning of February 7, 1985, attended by 230 schoolchildren. Before the Mass, a man later identified as Bryan Stanley, 29 years old, entered the sacristy and objected to the fact that sixth-grade girls would be reading at the Mass. He wanted to know who gave Father Rossiter permission to use females in the liturgy. Father Rossiter explained that the liturgical rules approved by the Holy See allowed girls and women to fulfill roles as readers and extraordinary ministers of the Eucharist. He suggested that if girl readers were upsetting, it might be best for the man to attend Mass elsewhere. The Mass was celebrated without incident, and no witness could recall Stanley being present.

After Mass the children returned to their classrooms, and Father Rossiter and Ferdinand Roth were in the sacristy when Stanley entered with a shotgun. He shot Father Rossiter in the face, and as Ferdinand Roth cried out for help, the lay minister was shot in the neck. William Hammes was shot in the face near the entrance of the church. All three shots were fatal. Stanley was arrested within minutes of the shooting, just blocks from the church, when a policeman saw him carrying a shotgun case. He was identified by parishioners as the man who had entered the sacristy, and by one parishioner who had seen him in the church with the shotgun. The funeral for the three slain men was held in St. Joseph the Workman Cathedral in La Crosse on February 11. The following day a service of reparation for violence was held in St. Patrick's Church so that it could be restored for use.

Source:
Times Review, La Crosse, Wisconsin, February 14, 1985

Indices

1. Alphabetical List
2. By Place of Death
3. By Religious Affiliation

Index 1
Alphabetical List of Martyrs

(Number refers to sketch of martyr; for abbreviations, see page 14, or pp. 178-180.)

Martyrs of the United States, Index 2 (a): Listings by States Where They Died

Martyrs of the United States Index 2 (b): Listings in Lands Outside the United States

BOLIVIA (1)
Kruegler, William Carl, 135

CHINA (8)
Cairns, Robert J., 126
Coveyou, Walter, 122
Donovan, Gerard A., 125
Ford, Francis Xavier, 134
Holbein, Godfrey, 124
Jensen, Benedict, 130
Rauschenbach, Otto A., 129
Seybold, Clement, 123

EL SALVADOR (4)
Clarke, Maura, 138
Donovan, Jean, 141
Ford, Ita, 139

Kazel, Dorothy, 140

GUATEMALA (2)
Miller, James, 143
Rother, Stanley (142)

HONDURAS (1)
Cypher, Casimir, 137

KOREA (3)
Brennan, Patrick T., 132
Byrne, Patrick J., 133
Maginn, James, 131

SOLOMON ISLANDS (2)
Duhamel, Arthur C., 127
Hennessey, James Gerard, 128

Index 3: U.S. Martyrs by Religious Affiliation